PENGUIN BOOKS

ALEXANDER THE GREAT

TANIA LOUISE GERGEL was born in 1972 and educated at Bristol University, University College London, and King's College London. She is currently lecturing in Greek language and literature at King's College London and her main research interests are ancient Greek philosophy and stylistics. As well as various articles, she is now working on a book entitled "Style and Argument: An Investigation of Plato's *Phaedo*," and is the co-translator of *The Greek Sophists*, published in Penguin Classics in 2003.

MICHAEL WOOD was educated at Manchester Grammar School and Oriel College, Oxford, where he did postgraduate research in Anglo-Saxon history. Since then he has worked as a journalist, broadcaster and filmmaker, with over sixty films to his name. He is a Fellow of the Royal Historical Society. His book *In the Footsteps of Alexander the Great*, based on his BBC TV series, was a number-one bestseller, and he is the author of *Shakespeare, His Life and Times*, which accompanies the similarly named BBC TV series. He lives in London with his wife and their two daughters.

Alexander the Great

Selected Texts from Arrian, Curtius and Plutarch

Edited by TANIA GERGEL
With an Introduction by MICHAEL WOOD

PENGUIN BOOKS

PENGUIN BOOKS

Published by the Penguin Group

Penguin Group (USA) Inc., 375 Hudson Street, New York, New York 10014, U.S.A.

Penguin Group (Canada), 10 Alcorn Avenue, Toronto,

Ontario, Canada M4V 3B2 (a division of Pearson Penguin Canada Inc.)

Penguin Books Ltd, 80 Strand, London WC2R 0RL, England

Penguin Ireland, 25 St Stephen's Green, Dublin 2, Ireland (a division of Penguin Books Ltd)

Penguin Group (Australia), 250 Camberwell Road, Camberwell,

Victoria 3124, Australia (a division of Pearson Australia Group Pty Ltd)

Penguin Books India Pvt Ltd, 11 Community Centre, Panchsheel Park, New Delhi – 110 017, India

Penguin Group (NZ), cnr Airborne and Rosedale Roads, Albany, Auckland,

New Zealand (a division of Pearson New Zealand Ltd)

Penguin Books (South Africa) (Pty) Ltd, 24 Sturdee Avenue, Rosebank,

Johannesburg 2196, South Africa

Penguin Books Ltd, Registered Offices:

80 Strand, London WC2R 0RL, England

First published in Great Britain by Penguin Books in 2004

Published in the United States of America by Penguin Books in 2004

1 3 5 7 9 10 8 6 4 2

Introduction copyright © Michael Wood, 2004

Extracts from Arrian, *The Campaigns of Alexander*,

first published in this translation 2004. Copyright © Tania Gergel, 2004

Extracts from Curtius, *The History of Alexander*, first published in this translation 1984,

revised 2001. Translation copyright © John Yardley, 1984, 2001

Extracts from Plutarch, *Alexander* first published in this translation 1973.

Translation copyright © Ian Scott-Kilvert, 1973

Additional material and notes copyright © Tania Gergel, 2004

All rights reserved

CIP data available

ISBN 0 14 20.0140 6

Printed in the United States of America

Set in PostScript Adobe Sabon

Contents

Chronology

328/327 Winter. Capture of Sisimithres' rock.
  Alexander marries Roxane.

327 Spring. Introduction of *proskynesis*.

326 May. Alexander at the Hydaspes; battle with Porus.
  Summer. Mutiny at the Hyphasis.
  Death of Coenus.

326/325 November 326–July 325. Descent of the Indus river
  system.

325 August. Alexander begins his return to the west.

325/324 Winter. Alexander in Carmania.

324 Summer. Meeting at Opis.
  Autumn. Death of Hephaestion.

323 May. The dinner party of Medius; Alexander falls ill.
  10 June. Alexander's death.

Introduction

The texts in this collection are drawn from three ancient biographies of Alexander of Macedonia – Alexander 'the Great' – who died in Babylon in 323 BC at the age of just thirty-two having conquered half of the known world. His is one of those stories in history that has had the power to captivate every generation. In the popular view Alexander achieved undying fame as history's golden boy, the ultimate hero endowed with youth, intellect and beauty who pursued an extraordinary destiny, only to burn out too soon. His image – hair like a lion's mane, head tilted to one side, melting eyes fixed on far horizons – has compounded this myth ever since his own day, even though we now know it was the creation of carefully controlled 'spin' like the airbrushing of a modern tyrant's photo. The real Alexander, so far as we can tell, was short and stocky, with a big nose, a large chin and small eyes. But the idea of his godlike beauty has been as hard to remove as the mythical dimensions of his heroic tale, a tale created originally by the companions who went with him in their now lost accounts. The eternal fascination with Alexander is not due only to the amazing events he set in motion, but also to the inextricable tangle of history and myth that surrounds him. As the Greeks said, 'Those whom the gods love die young.'

The Macedonians were a rugged people from the mountainous region of northern Greece. Alexander's father Philip had created the kingdom of Macedonia with a powerful army that crushed all opposition within Greece. At that time, just across the Aegean Sea, lay the western provinces of the Persian empire, the greatest power that had yet existed in the world. The Persian king, Darius, claimed a loose overlordship extending from Upper Egypt to the Indus, and as far north as the Syr-Darya river, on what is now the Tajik–Uzbek border, running into the Aral Sea from the Pamirs. Fabulously wealthy, when Alexander came to power the Persians exacted annual tribute from over thirty different nations. A hundred and fifty years earlier they had attempted to conquer Greece, only to be decisively defeated in battles in Salamis and Plataea. To the Greeks the Persian war represented a latterday heroic age; they had never forgotten the desecration of their temples, and there had long been talk of mounting a war of revenge.

Alexander became ruler of Macedonia at the age of nineteen, after his father's assassination. Two years later, in May 334, he set out on the great war of retribution against the Persians. Crossing the Hellespont into Asia, he paid his respects to the ghosts of the Greek heroes of Troy, who had died in what the Greeks saw as the first clash between East and West. Then Alexander's nine-year campaign began with an attack on Anatolia, to secure the Greek-speaking cities of what is now western Turkey. However, not all in the region regarded him as a liberator, and in places there was stiff resistance. In Greece, too, especially in Athens, many were hoping that the young 'mad hatter' would come unstuck. It is now clear how far he originally intended to go, but in late 333 he fought a great battle against Darius near Issus on the main trunk route into Syria. The next year he was occupied with lengthy and costly sieges at Tyre and Gaza on the Levant coast before heading into Egypt. There the native aristocracy seem to have accepted the Greeks with relief after their experience of Persian intolerance towards their own religion. It was at this point that Alexander made his famous journey to the oracle at Siwa in the Western Desert, where the priesthood greeted him as the son of Ammon, paving the way for him to be accepted as a legitimate pharaoh. The later Greek Alexander Romance, composed in Egypt in the first century BC, says he was crowned with traditional Egyptian ritual at Memphis. The march on Persia itself began in 332, and Alexander won a decisive battle at Tel Gomel (Gaugamela) near Irbil in Kurdistan on 1 October, after which Babylon and other great cities of Iraq, the centre of the ancient world, surrendered. Now he could call himself, as Darius had done, 'Lord of the World' – except that Darius himself was still at large.

Early in the following year, with his pan-Hellenic army now a massive 70,000 strong, Alexander fought his way with elite forces through the Zagros mountains in a desperate battle at a pass known to the Greeks as the Persian Gates. The Persian royal city of Parsa, Persepolis, was then taken intact with the royal treasures. From that moment the capture of the Persian king was only a matter of time. That summer Alexander made a lightning advance past Isfahan (Gabae) and then eastwards by the city of Rhagae (near today's Tehran), finally circling the Ahuran massif through the desert at night only to find Darius murdered by his own officers by a small pool on the Khorasan road just short of the city of Quse (Hecatompylos). From then on, even though opposition continued, Alexander was effectively ruler of the Persian empire, and came to act increasingly like a Persian king. The texts tell us that he demanded prostration and adoration, which may well have been expected in some of the conquered lands, but did not go down well with the old-fashioned veterans of the Macedonian officer corps. Inevitably, though, Iran was becoming the centre of Alexander's world; he would never see Greece again.

The next phase of the campaign took the Greeks to the Caspian Sea, into Afghanistan and over the Hindu Kush into Central Asia. Outlying forces seem to have penetrated as far as Bukhara and Merv (the future Alexandria-in-Margiana); the main army journeyed past Samarkand to the Syr-Darya river and the Mogul Tau Mountains. There, after two years of sapping warfare against local guerrillas, he negotiated a peace and marked the northern limit of his empire, believing himself to be close to the great ocean which Greek geographers thought circled the land mass of Europe, Asia and Africa.

In 327 BC, having taken the Bactrian princess Roxanne as his wife, he returned to the Kabul plain and prepared to invade India. The battle-hardened Greek army crossed the Khyber Pass and, after heavy fighting in the north-western frontier and the valley of the Swat, bridged the Indus and occupied the Indian city of Taxila. Moving further into the subcontinent, Alexander defeated the Raja of the Punjab, Porus, in a savage battle close to the modern town of Jalalpur on the river Jhelum. At this point, the heat, monsoon rains, disease and local resistance all began to erode morale. Alexander's march continued eastwards as far as the Beas river in the present-day Indian Punjab, in sight of the Himalayan foothills. There, after eight years' campaigning, the army showed its disinclination to go further, and the king grudgingly turned back (though it should not be forgotten that his successors penetrated down the Ganges as far as Patna). Alexander's return down the Indus valley involved more heavy fighting, the wholesale destruction of Indian cities, and a final nightmare journey through the Makran Desert into southern Iran. From then on, certainly with hindsight, his dream begins to unravel. We hear reports of drunkenness and get the impression of a lack of direction. The death of his favourite and lover – Hephaestion – after a massive binge seems to have led to fits of murderous fury and bouts of depression. Wounds and sickness had also no doubt taken their toll, and in 323 Alexander died in Babylon, probably from medical complications exacerbated by alcoholism, although there were persistent rumours that he had been poisoned by disenchanted members of his court.

What Alexander would have done had he lived is one of the great what-ifs of history. It seems likely that he had intended to return to India, and, according to the historian Diodorus of Sicily, his death prevented planned moves west into the Mediterranean and North Africa as far as the Atlantic. The expedition of a Massiliot navigator, Pytheas, who in 325 BC circumnavigated Britain, penetrated the Baltic and reached the ice floes around Iceland, gives some idea of the rapidly expanding knowledge of the world that was available to Alexander before he died. It has been conjectured that Pytheas' voyage was in some sense a Macedonian reconnaissance, and if Pytheas' account *On the Ocean* was in Alexander's hands in Babylon in 323, it would give some tantalizing substance to the idea recorded in Arrian that Alexander 'had he lived . . . would not have rested until he had subdued the world as far as the Britannic islands'.

Those are the bare bones of the story. It was by common consent one of the great episodes in the history of the world, an extraordinary tale of bravery and cruelty, endurance and excess, chivalry and greed; a journey of ten years and the best part of 20,000 miles all told. The empire broke up rapidly after Alexander's death, though Hellenistic kingdoms survived in places for centuries afterwards: the Seleucids in Babylonia, the Ptolemies in Egypt, of whom the Greek-speaking Cleopatra was the last, 300 years after Alexander. Out in the wilds of Afghanistan, Bactria and the Punjab, Indo-Greek kingdoms lasted a similar length of time, minting their coins in Greek on one side and in Indian script on the other, harking back with nostalgia to the days of 'Great Alexander'. (Kipling's *The Man Who Would Be King* is a last reverberation of that tale from the days of the British empire, when oral traditions of those fabled kingdoms survived among the pagans of the Hindu Kush.)

Alexander's empire left strange and glittering debris in its wake: lost cities, blue-eyed Indians, exotic treasures, ancient manuscripts, and a great harvest of stories, songs, poems, myths and legends. His legend spread to every corner of the Old World: Alexander appears in the apocalyptic visions of the biblical Book of Daniel as the 'Third Beast' who unleashes a bloody tide on humankind. In the Muslim Koran he is the mysterious 'Two-Horned One' who builds a magical wall to keep out Gog and Magog, the evil ones who will ravage the earth with Satan in the last days. There are over 200 different Alexander epics and poems in medieval European languages alone, surviving in literally thousands of manuscripts in Russian, Polish, Old French, Czech and Serbian, among others. In Jewish tradition Alexander is a folk hero: though he was a Gentile, his name may be given to orthodox Jewish boys. There is a medieval German Alexander epic, an Icelandic Alexander Saga, and an Ethiopian Alexander Romance. The modern Greek chapbook 'Alexander', which circulated under Turkish occupation, has been reprinted dozens of times in the last three centuries. You will find Alexander depicted as one of the four kings on the standard French pack of playing cards; you'll still find the map of his empire in every Greek school and, until recently, on every traditional taverna wall. He is on Sicilian carnival carts, Ethiopian bridal cloths, Byzantine church murals and in paintings from Moghul India. His tale was re-interpreted by every generation since his day. The Jews told how he punished the ten Lost Tribes of Israel and found the Wonderstone in the earthly paradise; Muslim poets told how he discovered the tree of everlasting life, plumbed the deepest sea in a diving bell, and rose to heaven on a magic chariot pulled by griffons. In Europe in the Middle Ages he was the 'perfect knight' and the philosopher-king, and the legend of his ascent to heaven, carved on cathedral stalls from Wells in Somerset to Otranto in southern Italy, became an anticipation of glory in the hereafter. Indian legend said he had found the Speaking Tree, which had foretold his destiny: 'To die young but win eternal glory.'

The fascination shows no sign of abating in recent years; indeed, there has been an unparalleled outpouring of books, monographs, novels and films on the king. At the start of the twenty-first century Hollywood has no less than three movie versions of Alexander's life in production. Throughout history, of course, people have always sought and found things in Alexander's life to mirror their own fantasies and desires. In Hitler's Germany the greatest Alexander scholar portrayed him as 'intellect and power', the Superman as real-life hero and model, the embodiment of manifest destiny. Conversely, in the latter days of the British empire, imperial historians like Sir William Tarn saw him as a visionary idealist, a benevolent empire builder in their own mould, pursuing the dream of uniting humankind under one rule, irrespective of race, creed or colour.

Now, at the troubled start of a new century, another Alexander is being disentangled from the sources, one who no doubt will be reflected in the new Hollywood versions just as Tarn's was in the Richard Burton film of 1956. Indeed, Alexander has perhaps never been the subject of such close scrutiny. The dark deeds of his reign are being investigated in the way that war crimes in Vietnam, Cambodia or Bosnia were. The Macedonian conquests, hitherto seen through Greek sources exclusively, are now being illuminated for the first time by native sources, newly discovered diaries, oracles and prophecies on papyrus or clay tablets. The Greek adventure in Asia is being reconsidered in terms of modern ideas on colonialism, orientalism and racism. So, too, the king's power politics – his purges and massacres; his reliance on intelligence, spies and secret police; his control of information, manipulation of images and production of state propaganda; his use of torture against opponents and terror against civilian populations – are now being seen in the light of modern authoritarian states. All these facts which are attested in our sources have taken on new meaning in our own time, which has lived through the great communist utopian tyrannies and their offshoots. On the other hand, our view of the material culture of his court, and that of his father Philip, has been dramatically widened by the sensational archaeological discoveries at the royal tombs at Vergina. There, for example, one eye-catching detail – the great collection of wine-mixing bowls, strainers and decanters – recalls the drinking culture of the royal circle so frequently described in our sources. The nature of the Macedonian religious cult in the king's lifetime has also recently been thrillingly illuminated by the remarkable recovery and reconstruction of the Derveni papyrus. On the king's sexuality there are new insights too, as more becomes known about Greek male attitudes to women and to homosexuality, and specifically about the importance of male love affairs in the internal politics and sometimes deadly jealousies and feuds of the Macedonian court. Others have attempted to look into the king's mind, in particular at the psychology of his leadership and the pitfalls of absolute power. A new study has suggested that alcoholism – days-long Dionysiac drinking bouts as the increasingly isolated and paranoid king followed ever more devotedly in his god's footsteps – was the root of his downfall. The most recent survey has found suggestive parallels with Cortes and the conquistadors, emphasizing the king's dark side, 'murderous and melancholy mad', as one hostile contemporary portrayed him. It's all a far cry from the golden boy we have heard about for so long; it may perhaps be nearer to his truth – but there is no doubt that it is nearer to ours.

The historical significance of the Greek adventure in Asia lies not in military events, however, but in the interaction of cultures over the following thousand years or more in the lands between India and the Mediterranean. Mingling with Egyptian, Arab, Indian, Iranian and Jewish culture, Greek art and thought accelerated and deepened the exchange of ideas in the old heartland of civilization. In some ways this was the first globalizing age: cosmopolitan, internationalizing and self-aware; fascinated like us by the possibilities of mimetic art, by sex, violence and the grotesque; and above all concerned with inquiring into the nature of humankind and the physical universe. These ideas rapidly spread beyond the bounds of the Hellenized world: the theorem of Pythagoras, for example, reached China within a couple of decades of the king's death. This mingling led to translations from Greek to Prakrit in north-western India in ancient times; and Greek culture and language would be key elements between the eastern Mediterranean and the Hindu Kush for a thousand years. It is often forgotten that Greek culture was a profound influence on many aspects of Islamic civilization in the Middle Ages. Greek medicine, philosophy and science remained on the curriculum of traditional Muslim colleges in Iraq, Iran and India well into our own time, and lost Greek texts in Persian or Arabic are still turning up in the libraries of the subcontinent. This galvanizing meeting of ideas created fascinating and original intellectual movements such as the Christian Origen in Egypt, or the Muslim Platonists in Shiite Islam.

So 'war drives all things', as the pre-Socratics said. The Hellenistic age led to a tremendous opening up of the world, and it is no coincidence that the three great internationalizing religions – Christianity, Manichaism and Islam – all rose during the Late Antique period in the Near East in the Greek culture zone. Jesus, Mani and Mohammed were all citizens of the multilingual post-Hellenistic world, in which Greek was the lingua franca. In the very heart of the Arabian peninsula, haunting wall paintings uncovered at the city of Faw show Hellenism inspiring the local civic culture before the time of the Prophet. One of the last Greek papyri from seventh-century AD Egypt, from the former temple town of Horus-Apollo at Edfu, is inscribed with the Muslim creed written in Greek.

None of these amazing developments could have been foreseen, of course, in 329 BC by Alexander and his generals as they stood gritting their teeth in the gale on the heights of the Hindu Kush, from where, his teacher Aristotle had taught him, it ought to have been possible to see the ends of the earth. Alexander started out aged nineteen driven by an appetite for fame and glory and, if the spin doctors' story is true, with Homer under his pillow and a determination to emulate the heroes and gods of the Trojan tale. In the end, if sources hostile to him can be believed, he sank into megalomaniac identification with those gods. How to get to know him is one of the great riddles raised by the texts in this collection. An official account of the expedition was produced; several combatants wrote memoirs, as did generals, surveyors and even scientists. But of them only fragments remain, quoted by later writers. As far as contemporary evidence goes, the most important is archaeological and epigraphic; for example, the ruins of the cities Alexander founded between Egypt and India, of which fascinating traces have been discovered in places as far away as Ai Khanoum on the Amu-Darya in northern Afghanistan (Alexandria on the Oxus).

The only full narratives we have – the main ones are in this book – are drawn from works written very late in the day as far as sources go: none is primary. Of the three excerpted here, it is actually the earliest that is the most sensational. Written in Latin by the Roman historian Curtius, who lived at the court of Nero in mid first century BC, it appeared, therefore, the best part of four centuries after the events it describes. But that is not the only problem. The surviving sources often illustrate opposite points of view. On the one hand, there is a cluster that is interested in painting the dark side of Alexander in often lurid terms, both in his private life, including his sexual proclivities, and in his conduct as a leader and a general. On the other hand, there are those who tend to see him as a noble soul who occasionally did bad things when under pressure. Both sides preserve valuable material from now lost early sources, but their differences in perspective make the task of discovering the 'real' Alexander – if such a thing is ever feasible – both difficult and enduringly fascinating.

The former group, known to the scholars as the 'vulgate' tradition consists of Curtius, Diodorus of Sicily, Justin, and an intriguing manuscript known as the Metz Epitome which, even though written in the tenth century AD, has interesting detail which is otherwise unrecorded, such as the death of Alexander's first child by Roxanne on the banks of the Jhelum in India. Plutarch also tends to be placed within this group, although his criticisms of Alexander are more reasoned and less sensational.

In the second group, much of the controversial detail is omitted or glossed over, especially Alexander's war crimes (for instance, the crucifixion of the survivors of the siege of Tyre, the sadistic killing of the enemy leader at Gaza, and above all the massacre of the Branchidae in Central Asia). The chief representative of this apologetic tradition is Arrian.

A former military man and a Greek speaker, Arrian was a provincial governor in the peaceful days of the Roman empire in the second century AD, so he was born 400 years after Alexander's death. He too lived far away, by the shores of the Sea of Marmara, so no more than Curtius had he the chance to see the places his hero visited 'spreading the power of his name over the whole earth'. However, for his account Arrian used earlier histories and journals of the expedition written by participants including Alexander's general Ptolemy, who took Egypt after Alexander's death and founded the last Egyptian royal dynasty. Arrian was unashamedly pro-Alexander. He tells us that the tale had captured his imagination from his youth. In his time, he says, as in our own, Alexander had run into the debunkers, and lurid tales like the brilliant novelistic narrative of Curtius, with their mix of plots and paranoia, drunkenness, sex and war crimes, had more popular appeal. Arrian's answer was to go back carefully to the primary sources, to try to sift the tale as judiciously and as fairly as he could. To be sure, he omitted some stories which reflected badly on his hero, but in the end he used his sources with critical acuity and a wealth of detail which perhaps makes his Alexander, for all its bias, the nearest we can hope to get to him this far on in time.

Arrian often preserves fascinatingly precise information which must ultimately come from on-the-spot observation by his sources. Following the route of Alexander on the ground with his text in hand in the late 1990s, I found parts of his narrative suddenly becoming crystal clear. For example, in his account of the dramatic battle for the Persian Gates (now conclusively identified as a pass in the Zagros called Tang e-Mohammed Reza), it became possible to see where, in his description of the decisive manoeuvres, Arrian had excerpted Ptolemy's own diary. Unexpectedly finding that the pass was defended, having been repulsed by the Persians in the narrows, Alexander embarked on a very risky turning movement through the night, using local guides to get round the back of the pass. In the middle of the night, Arrian says, Ptolemy was left on top on the high plateau above the pass with 3,000 troops which he was to bring down at dawn on to the 'middle of the defences'. The pass is six miles long, and in only one place, right behind the narrowest point, is there a break in the towering cliffs. There, a steep but walkable ravine comes right down from the plateau on to an open space which must have been at the back of the Persian defences. This is clearly where the Greeks came down that January in freezing darkness. (Curtius incidentally adds another precise eyewitness detail: during the turning manoeuvre that night at the top of the path the Greeks turned off *to the right* – which is true, and which must have also come from a first-hand report.) Reading these accounts while camped on the crags above the Persian Gates brought home vividly the layers of transmission which connect texts like Arrian's with the dramatic events of Alexander's expedition.

In Afghanistan, another tiny detail from Arrian illuminated a further crucial and dramatic moment in the story. Back in the winter of 330–329 BC, Alexander made a fast advance early in the new year to get forces over the Hindu Kush from the Kabul plain into the plain of the Oxus, in order to catch the Persian governor of Bactria unawares. The pass he took was almost certainly the Khawak, and Curtius paints a stark picture of the icy snow whipping off the peaks into the faces of the troops as they hunched their shoulders and trudged on into the blizzard. Many of the men were suffering from snow blindness and altitude sickness; all were hungry, and the king rode up and down the column encouraging them. Alexander's enemies, Arrian tells us, 'had laid waste the lands around the foot of the Hindu Kush mountains in the hope that if all the crops and everything edible were destroyed, Alexander would be stopped by sheer lack of supplies'. And so he might well have been. The land is high and barren; it was January, bitterly cold at night; and it took the army nearly three weeks to get over from front to tail. Provisions for an army that size would run into several tons – if they could find any. Inevitably, the army ran out of food, and the quartermasters asked for permission to start killing the pack animals. But there was no wood on these bare hills with which to make cooking fires, and the men were reduced to eating the flesh raw. To offset illness, Arrian says they used the juice of a plant which grew on the mountains and which he calls sylphion. Historians have often wondered about this tale. Puzzling over it as we climbed the Khawak, I questioned our horse handlers and they showed me the plant: with a big stem thick as your wrist, it grows in the early spring and is widely used as a medicine. In the Middle Ages it was produced in bulk and sold in the bazaars of Merv and Bukhara. Even during the Russian occupation, we were told, the mujahedin guerrillas used it to heal wounds and cure stomach upsets. A tiny detail, but one which shows the immediacy of the material on which Arrian was drawing.

What we also gained on the ground – and especially from his night marches at high altitude in pitch dark -- was of course an insight into Alexander's character. The implacable drive, remorseless, unstoppable; his 'incredible mental energy and almost excessive tolerance of fatigue' as Curtius says; what Arrian calls his *pothos*: his desire to win and excel, his drive. On that same journey across the Hindu Kush, at the top of the Khawak Pass, at a little under 12,000 feet, having laboured by

jeep and on foot from Kabul and up the Panjshir valley, it was
hard not to understand what Arrian meant. In a bitter wind,
with snow on the surrounding peaks and creamy-white clouds
sailing over the tops, we saw the view the Greeks had seen all
those years before, stood on the spot where Alexander had
stood. He knew now that he had got through; the gamble had
paid off: this time the pass was undefended. Below us, still sunlit,
the road snaked down towards northern Afghanistan and the
Oxus, beyond which lay the great plains of Central Asia, and,
for Alexander, the shore of the Great Ocean, the outermost edge
of the world – as he understood it.

'Nothing put him off,' says Arrian, 'at this moment his
enemies' hopes were in vain; in spite of everything, Alexander
just kept coming on and on. The freezing cold and the starvation
made it a tremendous task, but they couldn't stop him . . . And
in the end his enemies were struck with fear and amazement at
the speed of his advance'. Standing shivering on top of the
Khawak Pass as the sharp wind from Bactria beat in our faces,
it was easy to see why.

What also struck me was that at the very end of the twen-
tieth century, aspects of the legend of Alexander were still very
much alive. Travelling in his footsteps among oral cultures
not yet ruined by television and the globalization of ideas, we
became aware that Alexander's tale still reverberates across
much of Asia, especially in the Muslim world, where he is
still a great folk hero, whether 'The Two-Horned One', the
'Great', or even 'Alexander the Accursed' (as he is known to the
Zoroastrians in Iran). And the more we heard, the more we
came to realize that through our goal was to try to uncover the
real historical events, the legend was almost as powerful and
fascinating.

Many wars have little long-term effect. This one changed
the world between the Mediterranean and India. Alexander's
expedition was a turning point in human history; opening up
contacts between East and West, Europe and Asia, it laid the
foundations for much of what followed. Like the European
conquest of the Americas, it involved cruelty and destruction,

but it unleashed astonishing historical energies, in particular, the interaction of cultures whose effect is still to be felt today in the lands between the Mediterranean and the Himalayas. And, of course, through the Romans and their successors, the fruits of this great opening up were bequeathed to the western world too.

At the heart of this amazing and often terrible story is the enigmatic character of Alexander himself. Though he was only thirty-two when he died, there is still the widest disagreement on his true nature and motives, and no doubt there always will be. Short of finding the memoirs of one of his companions in an Egyptian papyrus dump, the last word will always rest with the historians whom you will find in these pages: Arrian, Curtius and Plutarch. Carrying their accounts with me in my rucksack, I came to enjoy them immensely both as literature and as travelling companions, and, reading them at night in tents, on riverboats and in station waiting rooms, I even felt I got to know them a little as people. All were citizens of the Roman empire, and of course that coloured each one's agenda: Plutarch, a priest at Delphi, humane and likeable, has an unerring eye for character – character as destiny; Arrian is a decent chap, an administrator, who, like Plutarch, believes in the basic goodness of the imperial project; Curtius an enigmatic member of Nero's court, is more interested in the corruptions of absolute power and in the darker side of human greatness.

When our own journey in Alexander's footsteps was over, I remember sitting sweltering in the little port of Gwadar, on the edge of the forbidding Makran Desert, which Alexander crossed on his desperate return from India. From a veranda I looked out to the Arabian Sea where Nearchus had sailed the Greek fleet from the Indus delta back to the Gulf, believing Alexander dead and his army destroyed. But as always, against the odds, Alexander got through: somewhere near Hormuz, unshaven and sunburnt, they embraced each other and cried tears of relief. As a wind hot as an oven swept in from the fiery gravel landscapes and sand dunes of the Makran, I turned to Arrian's last page:

'Anyone who belittles Alexander has no right to do so on the evidence only of what merits censure in him; he must base his criticism on a comprehensive view of his whole life and career ... It is my belief that ... never in the world was there another like him.'

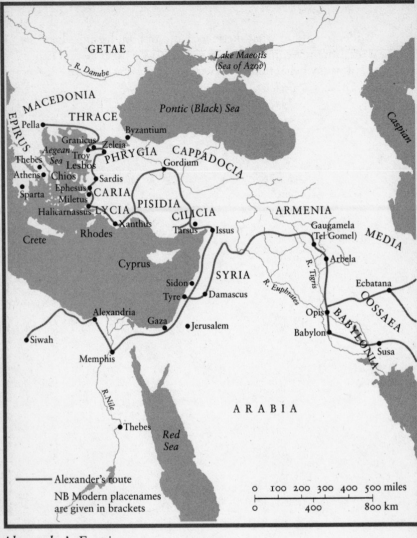

Alexander's Empire

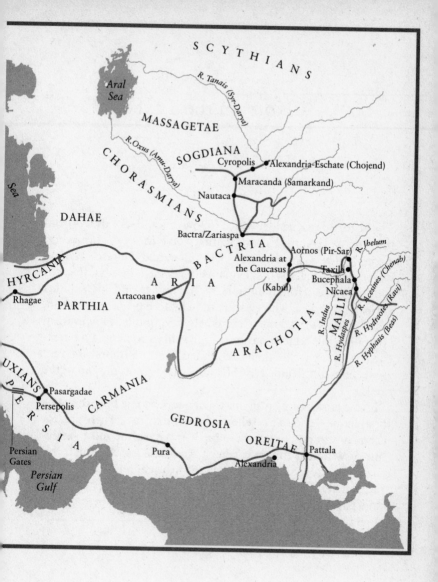

A Note on the Texts

The history of Alexander which follows comprises extracts from three texts: Quintus Curtius Rufus' *The History of Alexander*, Arrian's *The Campaigns of Alexander* and Plutarch's *Alexander*. As Michael Wood explains in his introduction, the attitude of each of these authors to Alexander and his exploits varies a great deal, with Curtius and Plutarch prone to criticism, while Arrian's account is extremely favourable. However, in compiling this edition our priority has been to maintain narrative continuity rather than to comment on the authors' different perspectives. A detailed list of sources is given at the end of the book.

In ancient Greece, as in our time, many people bore the same (first) name – and this is reflected in our excerpts. There are, for instance, several characters named Amyntas, the most significant of whom is Amyntas son of Andromedes. Although this may at first appear puzzling, generally the context will help the reader determine the identity of the person in question. The main participants in the story of Alexander told here can be found in the Glossary of Main Characters.

1. THE EARLY YEARS

Accounts of Alexander's youth tell of his auspicious birth, precocious ambition and ability. Lysimachus, Alexander's influential first tutor, calls Alexander Achilles, an association which remains with him throughout his exploits. Other famous episodes include his taming of the horse Bucephalus and the tutorship of Aristotle, the great Athenian philosopher. Demonstrating early skills in leadership, he holds the fort while his father, Philip, is on military campaigns. Yet, he is also wilful and fiercely loyal to his mother, Olympias, when Philip marries his second wife, Eurydice (Cleopatra). In summer 336, when Alexander is twenty, Philip is assassinated. The assassin, Pausanias, is duly punished, but it is generally believed that Olympias was behind the plot. After Philip's death, Alexander swiftly takes control as Olympias brutally removes the threat posed by the infant son of Eurydice.

On his father's side Alexander was descended from Hercules through Caranus, and on his mother's from Aeacus through Neoptolemus: so much is accepted by all authorities without question. It is said that his father Philip fell in love with Olympias, Alexander's mother, at the time when they were both initiated into the mysteries at Samothrace. He was then a young man and she an orphan, and after obtaining the consent of her brother Arybbas, Philip betrothed himself to her. On the night before the marriage was consummated, the bride dreamed that there was a crash of thunder, that her womb was struck by a thunderbolt, and that there followed a blinding flash from which a great sheet of flame blazed up and spread far and wide before it finally died away. Then, some time after their marriage, Philip saw himself in a dream in the act of sealing up his wife's womb, and upon the seal he had used there was engraved, so it seemed to him, the figure of a lion. The soothsayers treated this dream with suspicion, since it seemed to suggest that Philip needed to keep a closer watch on his wife. The only exception was Aristander of Telmessus, who declared that the woman must be pregnant, since men do not seal up what is empty, and that she would bring forth a son whose nature would be bold and lion-like. At another time a serpent was seen stretched out at Olympias' side as she slept, and it was this more than anything else, we are told, which weakened Philip's passion and cooled his affection for her, so from that time on he seldom came to sleep with her. The reason for this may either have been that he was afraid she would cast some evil spell or charm upon him or else that he recoiled from her embrace because he believed that she was the consort of some higher being.

However, there is another version of this story. It appears that from very ancient times all the women of this region have been initiates of the Orphic religion and of the orgiastic rites of Dionysus. For this reason they were known as Klodones and Mimallones and they followed many of the observances of the Edonian and Thracian women who live around Mount Haemus, from whom the word *threskeuein* has come to denote the celebration of extravagant and superstitious ceremonies. It was Olympias' habit to enter into these states of possession and surrender herself to the inspiration of the god with even wilder abandon than the others, and she would introduce into the festal procession numbers of large snakes, hand-tamed, which terrified the male spectators as they raised their heads from the wreaths of ivy and the sacred winnowing baskets, or twined themselves around the wands and garlands of the women.

At any rate, after Philip had seen this apparition he dispatched Chaeron of Megalopolis to Delphi to consult the oracle of Apollo. In reply the god commanded him to sacrifice to Zeus Ammon and to revere him above all other deities; but he also warned Philip that he was fated to lose the eye with which he had peered through the chink of the half-open door on the night when he saw the god in the form of a serpent sharing his wife's bed. According to Eratosthenes, Olympias, when she sent Alexander on his way to lead his great expedition to the East, confided to him and to him alone the secret of his conception and urged him to show himself worthy of his divine parentage. But other authors maintain that she repudiated this story and used to say, 'Will Alexander never stop making Hera jealous of me?'

However this may be, Alexander was born on the sixth day of the month Hecatombaeon, which the Macedonians call Loüs, the same day on which the temple of Artemis at Ephesus was burned down. It was this coincidence which inspired Hegesias of Magnesia to utter a joke which was flat enough to have put the fire out: he said it was no wonder the temple of Artemis was destroyed, since the goddess was busy attending to the birth of Alexander. But those of the Magi who were then at Ephesus interpreted the destruction of the temple as the portent of a far greater disaster, and they ran though the city beating their faces and crying out that that day had brought forth a great scourge and calamity for Asia.

At that moment Philip had just captured the city of Potidaea, and he received three messages on the same day. The first was that his general Parmenion had overcome the Illyrians in a great battle, the second that his race horse had won a victory in the Olympic games, and the third that Alexander had been born. Naturally he was overjoyed at the news, and the soothsayers raised his spirits still higher by assuring him that the son whose birth coincided with three victories would himself prove invincible.

The best likeness of Alexander which has been preserved for us is to be found in the statues sculpted by Lysippus, the only artist whom Alexander considered worthy to represent him. Alexander possessed a number of individual features which many of Lysippus' followers later tried to reproduce, for example the poise of the neck which was tilted slightly to the left, or a certain melting look in his eyes, and the artist has exactly caught these peculiarities. On the other hand, when Apelles painted Alexander wielding a thunderbolt, he did not reproduce his colouring at all accurately. He made Alexander's complexion appear too dark-skinned and swarthy, whereas we are told that he was fair-skinned, with a ruddy tinge that showed itself especially upon his face and chest. Aristoxenus also tells us in his memoirs that Alexander's skin was fresh and sweet-smelling, and that his breath and the whole of his body gave off a peculiar fragrance which permeated the clothes he wore.

The cause of this may have been the blend of hot and dry elements which were combined in his constitution, for fragrance, if we are to believe Theophrastus, is generated by the action of heat upon moist humours. This is why the hottest and driest regions of the earth produce the finest and most numerous spices, for the sun draws up the moisture which abounds in vegetable bodies and causes them to decay. In Alexander's case it was this same warmth of temperament which made him fond of drinking, and also prone to outbursts of choleric rage.

Even while he was still a boy, he gave plenty of evidence of his powers of self-control. In spite of his vehement and impulsive nature, he showed little interest in the pleasures of the senses and indulged in them only with great moderation, but his passionate desire for fame implanted in him a pride and a grandeur of vision which went far beyond his years. And yet it was by no means every kind of glory that he sought, and, unlike his father, he did not seek it in every form of action. Philip, for example, was as proud of his powers of eloquence as any sophist, and took care to have the victories won by his chariots at Olympia stamped upon his coins. But Alexander's attitude is made clear by his reply to some of his friends, when they asked him whether he would be willing to compete at Olympia, since he was a fine runner. 'Yes,' he answered, 'if I have kings to run against me.' He seems in fact to have disapproved of the whole race of trained athletes. At any rate, although he founded a great many contests of other kinds, including not only the tragic drama and performances on the flute and the lyre, but also the reciting of poetry, fighting with the quarter-staff and various forms of hunting, yet he never offered prizes either for boxing or for the *pancration*.*

* A contest which combined wrestling and boxing.

On one occasion some ambassadors from the king of Persia arrived in Macedonia, and since Philip was absent, Alexander received them in his place. He talked freely with them and quite won them over, not only by the friendliness of his manner, but also because he did not trouble them with any childish or trivial inquiries, but questioned them about the distances they had travelled by road, the nature of the journey into the interior of Persia, the character of the king, his experience in war, and the military strength and prowess of the Persians. The ambassadors were filled with admiration. They came away convinced that Philip's celebrated astuteness was as nothing compared to the adventurous spirit and lofty ambitions of his son. At any rate, whenever he heard that Philip had captured some famous city or won an overwhelming victory, Alexander would show no pleasure at the news, but would declare to his friends, 'Boys, my father will forestall me in everything. There will be nothing great or spectacular for you and me to show the world.' He cared nothing for pleasure or wealth but only for deeds of valour and glory, and this was why he believed that the more he received from his father, the less would be left for him to conquer. And so every success that was gained by Macedonia inspired in Alexander the dread that another opportunity for action had been squandered on his father. He had no desire to inherit a kingdom which offered him riches, luxuries and the pleasures of the senses: his choice was a life of struggle, of wars and of unrelenting ambition.

It was natural, of course, that a great number of nurses, pedagogues and teachers were appointed to take part in his upbringing, but the man who supervised them all was Leonidas, a severe disciplinarian, who was also a relative of Olympias. Although his duties were both important and honourable, he did not disdain the title of pedagogue, but because of his natural dignity and of his connection with the queen's family, other people referred to him as Alexander's foster-father and mentor. The person who took on both the title and the role of pedagogue was an Acarnanian named Lysimachus. He was neither an educated nor a cultivated man, but he managed to ingratiate himself by calling Philip Peleus, Alexander Achilles and himself Phoenix, and he held the second place in the prince's household.

There came a day when Philoneicus the Thessalian brought Philip a horse named Bucephalus, which he offered to sell for thirteen talents.* The king and his friends went down to the plain to watch the horse's trials, and came to the conclusion that he was wild and quite unmanageable, for he would allow no one to mount him, nor would he endure the shouts of Philip's grooms, but reared up against anyone who approached him. The king became angry at being offered such a vicious animal unbroken, and ordered it to be led away. But Alexander, who was standing close by, remarked, 'What a horse they are losing, and all because they don't know how to handle him, or dare not try!' Philip kept quiet at first, but when he heard Alexander repeat these words several times and saw that he was upset, he asked him, 'Are you finding fault with your elders because you think you know more than they do, or can manage a horse better?' 'At least I could manage this one better,' retorted Alexander. 'And if you cannot,' said his father, 'what penalty will you pay for being so impertinent?' 'I will pay the price of the horse,' answered the boy. At this the whole company burst out laughing, and then as soon as the father and son had settled the terms of the bet, Alexander went quickly up to Bucephalus, took hold of his bridle and turned him towards the sun, for he had noticed that the horse was shying at the sight of his own shadow, as it fell in front of him and constantly moved whenever he did. He ran alongside the animal for a little way, calming him down by stroking him, and then, when he saw he was full of spirit and courage, he quietly threw aside his cloak and with a light spring vaulted safely on to his back. For a little while he kept feeling the bit with the reins, without jarring or tearing his mouth, and got him collected. Finally, when he saw that the horse was free of his fears and impatient to show his speed, he gave him his head and urged him forward, using a commanding voice and a touch of the foot.

* In the extracts used in this book, currency is referred to by Greek, Roman and Persian names, depending on the preference of the author.

At first Philip and his friends held their breath and looked on in an agony of suspense, until they saw Alexander reach the end of his gallop, turn in full control and ride back, triumphant and exulting in his success. Thereupon the rest of the company broke into loud applause, while his father, we are told, actually wept for joy, and when Alexander had dismounted he kissed him and said, 'My boy, you must find a kingdom big enough for your ambitions. Macedonia is too small for you.'

Philip had noticed that his son was self-willed, and that while it was very difficult to influence him by force, he could easily be guided towards his duty by an appeal to reason, and he therefore made a point of trying to persuade the boy rather than giving him orders. Besides this he considered that the task of training and educating his son was too important to be entrusted to the ordinary run of teachers of poetry, music and general education: it required, as Sophocles puts it

> The rudder's guidance and the curb's restraint,

and so he sent for Aristotle, the most famous and learned of the philosophers of his time, and rewarded him with the generosity that his reputation deserved. Aristotle was a native of the city of Stageira, which Philip had himself destroyed. He now repopulated it and brought back all the citizens who had been enslaved or driven into exile.

He gave Aristotle and his pupil the temple of the Nymphs near Mieza as a place where they could study and converse, and to this day they show you the stone seats and shady walks which Aristotle used. It seems clear too that Alexander was instructed by his teacher not only in the principles of ethics and politics, but also in those secret and more esoteric studies which philosophers do not impart to the general run of students, but only by word of mouth to a select circle of the initiated. Some years later, after Alexander had crossed into Asia, he learned that Aristotle had published some treatises dealing with these esoteric matters, and he wrote to him in blunt language and took him to task for the sake of the prestige of philosophy. This was the text of his letter:

Alexander to Aristotle, greetings. You have not done well to
write down and publish those doctrines you taught me by word
of mouth. What advantage shall I have over other men if these
theories in which I have been trained are to be made common
property? I would rather excel the rest of mankind in my knowledge of what is best than in the extent of my power. Farewell.

Aristotle wished to encourage this ambition of his pupil's and
so when he replied to justify his action, he pointed out that these
so-called oral doctrines were in a sense both published and not
published. For example, it is true that his treatise on metaphysics
is written in a style which makes it useless for those who wish
to study or teach the subject from the beginning: the book serves
simply as a memorandum for those who have already been
taught its general principles.

It was Aristotle, I believe, who did more than anyone to
implant in Alexander his interest in the art of healing as well as
that of philosophy. He was not merely attracted to the theory
of medicine, but was in the habit of tending his friends when
they were sick and prescribing for them various courses of
treatment or diet, as we learn from his letters. He was also
devoted by nature to all kinds of learning and was a lover of
books. He regarded the *Iliad* as a handbook of the art of war
and took with him on his campaigns a text annotated by Aristotle, which became known as 'the casket copy', and which he
always kept under his pillow together with his dagger. When
his campaigns had taken him far into the interior of Asia and
he could find no other books, he ordered his treasurer Harpalus
to send him some. Harpalus sent him the histories of Philistus,
many of the tragedies of Aeschylus, Sophocles and Euripides,
and the dithyrambic poems of Telestes and Philoxenus.

At first Alexander greatly admired Aristotle and became more
attached to him than to his father, for the one, he used to say,
had given him the gift of life, but the other had taught him how
to live well. But in later years he came to regard Aristotle
with suspicion. He never actually did him any harm, but his
friendship for the philosopher lost its original warmth and
affection, and this was a clear proof of the estrangement which

developed between them. At the same time Alexander never lost the devotion to philosophy which had been innate in him from the first, and which matured as he grew older: he proved this on many occasions, for example by the honours which he paid to Anaxarchus, the fifty talents which he presented to Xenocrates, and the encouragement which he lavished upon Dandamis and Calanus.

While Philip was making an expedition against Byzantium, Alexander, although he was only sixteen years old, was left behind as regent of Macedonia and keeper of the royal seal. During this period he defeated the Maedi, who had risen in revolt, captured their city, drove out its barbarous inhabitants, established a colony of Greeks assembled from various regions, and named it Alexandroupolis. He also took part in the battle against the combined armies of Greece at Chaeronea,* and it is said to have been the first to break the line of the Theban Sacred Band.† Even in my own time an oak tree used to be pointed out near the river Cephisus which was known as Alexander's oak, because his tent had been pitched beside it at that time, and not far away is the mass grave of the Macedonians who fell in the battle. Because of these achievements Philip, as was natural, became extravagantly fond of his son, so much so that he took pleasure in hearing the Macedonians speak of Alexander as their king and Philip as their general.

But before long the domestic strife that resulted from Philip's various marriages and love affairs caused the quarrels which took place in the women's apartments to infect the whole kingdom, and led to bitter clashes and accusations between father and son. This breach was widened by Olympias, a woman of a jealous and vindictive temper, who incited Alexander to oppose his father. Their quarrel was brought to a head on the occasion of the wedding of Cleopatra, a girl with whom Philip had fallen in love and whom he had decided to marry, although she was far too young for him. Cleopatra's uncle Attalus, who had drunk

---

* In 338 BC, a decisive victory against the allied forces of Athens and Thebes for Philip, resulting in the subjection of the city states to the Macedonians.
† An entire military squadron of 300 men.

too much at the banquet, called upon the Macedonians to pray
to the gods that the union of Philip and Cleopatra might bring
forth a legitimate heir to the throne. Alexander flew into a rage
at these words, shouted at him, 'Villain, do you take me for a
bastard, then?' and hurled a drinking cup at his head. At this
Philip lurched to his feet, and drew his sword against his son,
but fortunately for them both he was so overcome with drink
and with rage that he tripped and fell headlong. Alexander
jeered at him and cried out, 'Here is the man who was making
ready to cross from Europe to Asia, and who cannot even cross
from one table to another without losing his balance.' After this
drunken brawl Alexander took Olympias away and settled her
in Epirus, while he himself went to live in Illyria.

Meanwhile Demaratus the Corinthian came to visit Philip.
He was an old friend of the Macedonian royal family and so
was privileged to speak freely. After the formal greetings and
courtesies had been exchanged, Philip asked him whether the
various city states of Greece were at harmony with one another.
Demaratus retorted, 'It is all very well for you to show so
much concern for the affairs of Greece, Philip. How about the
disharmony you have brought about in your own household?'
This reply sobered Philip to such an extent that he sent for
Alexander, and with Demaratus' help persuaded him to return.

In the following year Pixodarus, the satrap of Caria, tried
to form a family union with Philip, hoping by this means to in-
sinuate himself into a military alliance. His plan was to offer the
hand of his eldest daughter to Philip's son Arrhidaeus, and he
sent Aristocritus to Macedonia to try to negotiate the match.
Alexander's mother and his friends sent him a distorted account
of this manoeuvre, making out that Philip was planning to
settle the kingdom upon Arrhidaeus by arranging a brilliant
marriage and treating him as a person of great consequence.
Alexander was disturbed by these stories and sent Thessalus,
the tragic actor, to Caria to tell Pixodarus that he should pay
no attention to Arrhidaeus, who was not only an illegitimate
son of Philip's but was weak-minded as well: instead, he should
offer his daughter's hand to Alexander.

Pixodarus was far more pleased with this suggestion than

with his original proposal. When Philip discovered this, he went to Alexander's room, taking with him Philotas the son of Parmenion, one of the prince's companions. There he scolded his son and angrily reproached him for behaving so ignobly and so unworthily of his position as to wish to marry the daughter of a mere Carian, who was no more than the slave of a barbarian king. As for Thessalus, he wrote to the Corinthians ordering them to send him to Macedonia in chains, and at the same time he banished four of Alexander's friends, Harpalus, Nearchus, Erygius and Ptolemy. Later Alexander recalled all of these men and raised them to the highest honours.

Not long afterwards a Macedonian named Pausanias assassinated the king: he did this because he had been humiliated by Attalus and Cleopatra and could get no redress from Philip. It was Olympias who was chiefly blamed for the assassination, because she was believed to have encouraged the young man and incited him to take his revenge. It was said that when Pausanias met the young prince and complained to him of the injustice he had suffered, Alexander quoted the verse from Euripides' *Medea* in which Medea is said to threaten

The father, bride and bridegroom all at once.

However this may be, he took care to track down and punish those who were involved in the plot, and he showed his anger against Olympias for the horrible revenge which she took upon Cleopatra during his absence. (Plutarch)

2. ESTABLISHING POWER IN MACEDONIA, GREECE AND NORTHERN EUROPE

As the new king of Macedonia, the twenty-year-old Alexander immediately sets about re-establishing his father's control over Greece and northern Europe in a campaign which shows his abilities as a leader, in spite of his youth. However, he does encounter resistance, notably from Thebes, one of the key powers in Greece, which he swiftly defeats, destroying the city and selling almost all of the surviving citizens into slavery. After the sack of Thebes, Athens is quick to surrender. Only Sparta, the major remaining power in Greece, maintains its independence from Macedonian rule.

Alexander was only twenty years old when he inherited his kingdom, which at that moment was beset by formidable jealousies and feuds, and external dangers on every side. The neighbouring barbarian tribes were eager to throw off the Macedonian yoke and longed for the rule of their native kings: as for the Greek states, although Philip had defeated them in battle, he had not had time to subdue them or accustom them to his authority. He had swept away the existing governments, and then, having prepared their peoples for drastic changes, had left them in turmoil and confusion, because he had created a situation which was completely unfamiliar to them. Alexander's Macedonian advisers feared that a crisis was at hand and urged the young king to leave the Greek states to their own devices and refrain from using any force against them. As for the barbarian tribes, they considered that he should try to win back their allegiance by using milder methods, and forestall the first signs of revolt by offering them concessions. Alexander, however, chose precisely the opposite course, and decided that the only way to make his kingdom safe was to act with audacity and a lofty spirit, for he was certain that if he were seen to yield even a fraction of his authority, all his enemies would attack him at once. (Plutarch)

Alexander went into the Peloponnese and, having assembled the Peloponnesian Greeks, asked them to grant him the leadership of the Persian campaign, which they had already granted to Philip. His request was accepted by all but the Spartans, who answered that the way of their country was not to be led by others but to lead others themselves. There was also slight resistance from Athens; but the Athenians faltered as soon as Alexander approached, and agreed to grant him an even greater power than they had given to Philip. Alexander then returned to Macedonia to prepare for his Asian expedition.

In the spring he advanced into Thrace against the Triballians and Illyrians, as he had heard that they were causing some disturbance. Given that both were neighbouring countries, he thought it would be a bad idea to set off on a journey that would take him so far away from home without completely suppressing them first. From Amphipolis he began his invasion of Thrace, the land of those known as the 'independent Thracians', with Philippi and Mount Orbelus on his left. Next, we are told, he crossed the river Nestus and arrived, ten days later, at Mount Haemus. Here, in the narrow pass on the approaches of the mountain, he was met by a large number of armed locals and independent Thracians, who had positioned themselves higher on the slopes of Haemus over which the army needed to proceed and were preparing to block its advance. They had gathered together some carts and laid them just below them on the slopes, to use as a defensive fortification if they were attacked. At the same time, they had it in mind to throw the carts at the Macedonian phalanx as it climbed the steepest part of the mountain, in the belief that the close order of the men when the descending carts hit would make them more vulnerable to the force of the impact.

Alexander now had to decide on the safest manner to cross

the ridge. He realized that he would have to take this risk, as there was no other way round, and so he gave the order that, wherever the carts reached them, any of the infantry who were on flat ground and therefore had the space to break formation should do so to let the carts pass through. As for those who were constrained by the mountain, they should gather together, and some of them should fall to the ground with shields held closely linked above themselves, so that – as seemed plausible – the carts bearing down on them might be carried over them by their impetus and continue without harming them. And this is how it turned out, just as Alexander had ordered and expected. Some of the men broke rank, while the carts rolled down over the shields of the others, leaving them unscathed. In fact, not one person died underneath the carts.

Seeing that the carts which they had feared so much had passed without causing them any damage, they took courage and, with a cry, charged against the Thracians. Alexander told the archers from the right wing to move in front of the main phalanx, a more convenient position, and to shoot at the Thracians each time they attacked. He then placed himself at the head of his other troops and shield-bearers and of the Agrianes and led them to the left, where the archers were now targeting Thracian advances to hold them back. As the phalanx moved in close, they drove the lightly clothed and poorly armed enemy from their position without difficulty, so that they no longer waited for Alexander as he came in from the left but, flinging down their arms, fled down the mountain whenever they had a chance. Around 1,500 of them died, and only a few were taken alive: the rest were too quick and had too good a local knowledge. However, all the women who had been attending the men were captured, as were their children and their provisions.

Alexander, handing the booty over to Lysanias and Philotas, sent it back to the coastal cities, where they would distribute it. He then went on through Haemus to the Triballians and arrived at the river Lyginus, a three-day march from the Danube as you come to Haemus. Syrmus, the king of the Triballians, who had known about Alexander's march for some time, sent the Triballian women and children to the Danube and ordered them to cross the river to one of the islands in the river, called Peuce. It was to this island that the Triballians' Thracian neighbours had fled as Alexander approached. Syrmus and his men had also escaped here with them, but most of the Triballians had then fled back to the river from which Alexander had set off the day before.

When he learnt of their movements Alexander turned back to confront the Triballians and found that they were already setting up camp. Caught in this way, they regrouped in the grove by the river, while Alexander himself, having drawn up his phalanx into a tightly ordered formation, told the archers and slingers to aim their arrows and stones at the tribesmen to try to bring them out from the grove into the open. When the missiles came in range of them, the latter rushed out to attack the archers intending to enter into close combat with them, as archers have no armour. Having thus enticed the Triballians out of the grove, Alexander instructed Philotas to take the upper Macedonian cavalry and attack on their right wing, where they had advanced furthest as they rushed out, while he ordered Heracleides and Sopolis to lead the cavalry from Bottiaea and Amphipolis against the left wing. He led the phalanx of foot soldiers and the rest of the cavalry, which he had sent out in front of the phalanx, against the enemy's central ranks.

As long as the battle remained at long range, the Triballians held their ground; but, when the massed phalanx made a powerful charge at them and the cavalry fell upon them in all directions, not with spears, but thrusting at them with their very horses, they then turned back through the grove to the river. Three thousand perished in the escape, while few of them were taken alive, the dense wood along the river and nightfall preventing the Macedonians from making a thorough search. Ptolemy says that, of the Macedonians themselves, eleven cavalry and roughly forty infantry were killed.

Three days after the battle, Alexander arrived at the river Danube. This, the largest of the European rivers, passed through the greatest territories, dividing very warlike tribes: mainly Celts – it is from their land that the river's springs rise – of whom the most remote are the Quadi and the Marcomanni; then there is a branch of the Sauromatae, the Iazyges; then the Getae, who claim to have the gift of immortality; then the majority of the Sauromatae; then the Scythians as far as the estuary, where the river flows out through five mouths into the Black Sea. Here, Alexander found warships which had come downstream from Byzantium by way of the Black Sea. Filling them with archers and armed infantry, he sailed against the island where the Triballians and Thracians had fled and tried to land by force. However, wherever the ships landed along the river, the enemy attacked; the ships themselves were only few in number and did not contain many troops; most of the island was too steep to land on; and the river's current passing close to the island through the narrows, was swift and made it hard to navigate.

In response to this, Alexander withdrew the ships and decided to cross the Danube and to attack the Getae, who dwelt on the other side of the river. He had seen a large number of them, about 4,000 cavalry and 10,000 infantry, gathered on the riverbank, making preparations to repel a crossing, but he was also prompted by a desire to go to that side of the Danube, and actually joined the fleet himself. He had the leather covers which they used for tents filled with hay, and all the dug-out boats collected from the countryside – there was a good supply of these, as those who lived beside the Danube used them for fishing on the river, for travelling upstream to visit each other, or, very often, when they went on plundering expeditions. Having gathered together as many of these boats as possible he transported across the river as much of his army as could be done by this means. About 15,000 cavalry and 4,000 foot soldiers crossed the Danube with Alexander.

They made their crossing during the night, landing into a deep cornfield, which gave them good cover as they kept close to the bank. Around dawn Alexander led his men through the field, ordering his foot soldiers to bend the corn with the flat of their spears, on to untilled ground. While the phalanx were advancing through the field, the cavalry followed; but as they emerged from the crops, Alexander led the cavalry to the right wing and ordered Nicanor to lead the foot soldiers out in a square formation.

The Getae could not even withstand the first cavalry charge. Alexander's daring – the fact that he had so easily crossed the Danube, the greatest of rivers, in a single night, without a bridge over the strait – seemed incredible to them; and the massed ranks of the phalanx, together with the violence of the charge, struck terror into their hearts. First of all they fled to the city, which was about four miles away from the Danube. Then, when they saw that Alexander was leading his phalanx along the river, so that the infantry would not be caught in an ambush by the Getae, and that the cavalry were down in front, the Getae left their poorly fortified city and, with as many of the women and children on horses could be managed, headed off into the desert, as far away as possible from the city. Alexander took the city, and seized the valuables that the Getae had left behind. He handed the plunder over to Meleager and Philip to take back with them and razed the city himself, before sacrificing on the banks of the Danube to Zeus the Saviour, to Hercules, and even to the Danube itself, as it had not hindered him. That same day he led all of his men safely back to camp.

At this point, envoys came to Alexander from all the other self-governing tribes who lived along the Danube and from Syrmus, king of the Triballians. Some also came from the Celts who inhabit the Ionian gulf – a tall and proud people. All of them expressed their wish for the friendship of Alexander and he pledged his friendship to all, while they offered theirs in return. Then he asked the Celts what it was that they dreaded most out of all mortal things, hoping that his own great name had reached them, or even further, and that they would say that it was him who they feared most terribly of all. However, the Celts did not answer according to his expectations, for they inhabited an impenetrable land far away from Alexander, and realized that his mission lay elsewhere. So they said that they were fearful lest the sky should fall upon them. Yet he named them as his friends and made them allies before sending them home, simply remarking on their self-confidence.

Alexander then went on towards the country of Agrianes and the Paiones, where messengers came to him to announce that Cleitus, the son of Bardylis, had revolted and that he had been joined by Glaucias, the king of the Taulantians. They then informed him that the Autariates were ready to attack him as he marched. In response, he decided to set off as soon as possible. Langaros, king of the Agrianes, who had shown some affection for Alexander and had been on a private embassy to him even while Philip was still alive, was also with him now, accompanied by his bodyguard, the very finest and best-armed troops he possessed. When he learnt that Alexander was making enquiries about the Autariates as to who they were and how large their numbers, he replied that Alexander should not be concerned about them, as they were the least warlike people in the area. He suggested invading their country himself, to keep them occupied with their own affairs. Alexander consented to the attack and Langaros launched an invasion with devastating results for the Autariates. Thus the Autariates had their own problems to contend with, while Langaros was greatly honoured by Alexander and received those gifts which are most highly esteemed in the Macedonian court. Alexander even agreed that Langaros should marry his sister Cyna when he arrived in Pella. However, when Langaros returned home, he grew ill and died.

Alexander marched along the river Erigon, towards Pelium, a city now occupied by Cleitus, since it was the finest stronghold in the area. When he arrived there Alexander set up camp by the river Eordaicus and decided to launch his assault on the following day. However, Cleitus' men had control of the imposing and thickly wooded heights which ringed the city, and was therefore in a good position to strike at the Macedonians from every side, if they attacked. Glaucias, king of the Taulantians, was not yet present. As Alexander advanced against the city, the enemy first sacrificed three boys, three girls and three black rams, and then set off to meet the Macedonians in close combat. Nevertheless, as the two sides came together, the enemy withdrew from the powerful positions which they had occupied, leaving their sacrificial victims just lying there.

Now that he had the enemy confined within the city, Alexander positioned his men by the wall making preparations for a blockade; but on the next day the Taulantian king Glaucias arrived with a large force. Aware that a large number of warriors had fled inside the city and that Glaucias' massive army would attack the moment he stormed the fortifications, Alexander abandoned his plan to take the city with his small number of men. Instead, he sent Philotas off to forage, with as many of the cavalry as were necessary for protection, and with the pack animals from the camp. When Glaucias learnt about Philotas' expedition he marched out to attack them and took control of the high ground around the plain where Philotas' men were intending to look for food. Then Alexander, knowing the danger which would face his men and pack animals at nightfall, rushed to their aid himself, taking his bodyguard, his archers, the Agrianes and 400 cavalry. He left the remainder of the force by the city, lest, by withdrawing his entire army, he should allow the men inside the city to charge out and join Glaucias' forces. As for Glaucias, he deserted the high ground the moment he saw Alexander approaching, while the men with Philotas got safely back to camp. Nevertheless, Cleitus' and Glaucias' troops seemed to have caught Alexander in a difficult position: they held the commanding heights with a strong cavalry, and together had many javelin and sling-bearers, as well as a considerable number of foot soldiers; the men occupying the city were ready to attack Alexander's troops if they withdrew; and, finally, it appeared that the area of country through which the latter needed to negotiate their way was wooded and confined, a river running to one side of it, while on the other side rose the steep foothills of a high mountain: even with the shield-bearers four abreast, the army would not be able to pass through.

Faced by this situation, Alexander drew up his army into a phalanx 120 deep and placed 200 cavalry on each side of it, with an order to keep silent which the men swiftly obeyed. He instructed the heavy infantry first to raise their spears upright, and then, at his signal, to bring them back down ready for attack, inclining the mass of their spears to the right and then to the left. The phalanx itself he moved quickly forward and guided in several directions on either wing, arranging it into various formations in a short space of time, before grouping it into a wedge on the left side and leading it out against the enemy. For some time now, the enemy had been in a state of amazement as they watched the speed and order of the manoeuvres, and they did not wait for Alexander's men to approach, but deserted the first ridges. Alexander next ordered his Macedonians to raise the war-cry and beat their shields with their spears. Even more terrified by this noise, the Taulantians swiftly led their army back to the city.

Alexander then saw that only a few men held the hill along which he had to pass, so he ordered his Companions and personal Guard to take their shields and mount their horses to charge against them. If, when they reached the hill, the men who had occupied it were still there, half of the soldiers should dismount and fight on foot in among the cavalry. The enemy, however, anticipating Alexander's onslaught, abandoned the hill and fled on all sides into the mountains. Alexander then took possession of the hill with his Companions, sending for the Agrianes and archers, who numbered about 2,000. He ordered the Guard to cross the river, followed by the lines of Macedonian soldiers, and, once across, to spread out to the left, so that a dense phalanx would appear as soon as they had reached the opposite bank. He then kept guard from the hill, looking out for enemy movement.

When they saw the forces crossing the river, the enemy came from the mountains to attack the men who remained with Alexander, who were the last to depart; but as they drew near, Alexander was already rushing out at them with his troops while the main phalanx raised the battle-cry as they came back across the river to join them. Under their onslaught, the enemy yielded and fled, and Alexander ordered the Agrianes and the archers to hurry to the river. He himself overtook them and crossed first, but then saw that the enemy were pressing upon those at the rear. So, having set up his artillery on the bank, he gave the order that the siege engines should fire all available missiles as far as possible, while the archers, who were already halfway across the river, should shoot from their position. Glaucias' men didn't dare venture within range of the missiles. Meanwhile, the Macedonians crossed the river safely, so that not a single man died during the withdrawal.

Three days later Alexander found out that the men with

Cleitus and Glaucias had set up camp carelessly, and that not only were no sentries in place to guard them, but they had not built a palisade, nor dug a trench, for they believed that Alexander had withdrawn in fear; furthermore, they had extended their line too far for safety. Hidden by the night, he crossed the river back again, taking his Guards, the Agrianes and the troops of Perdiccas and Coenus along with him. He instructed the rest of the army to follow, but then saw that it was an opportune moment to strike and, without waiting for them all to gather, sent forth the archers and Agrianes. They made an unexpected attack with the phalanx ordered in narrow formation, which allowed them to make their strongest assault against the enemy at its weakest point. Some they slaughtered in their beds, while they easily caught those who were fleeing, so that many were seized and killed on the spot, and many others as they withdrew in disorder and fear, although quite a few were taken alive. Alexander's men pursued them as far as the mountains of the Taulantians, and those who escaped only saved themselves by discarding their weapons. As for Cleitus, he first fled to the city, but then set it alight and withdrew with Glaucias in Taulantian territory.

Meanwhile some of the Theban exiles fled back to Thebes during the night, invited by certain people whose intention was to cause an uprising in the city. They seized and killed Amyntas and Timolaus from among those who were occupying the Cadmeia, who had no suspicion of any hostility against them. Then they came before the Assembly to urge the Thebans to break away from Alexander, proposing 'freedom' and 'self-rule', those fine and ancient words, along with release, at last, from Macedonian oppression. To the majority they seemed even more persuasive when they insisted that Alexander had died in Illyria, repeating what was a popular and widespread rumour. Alexander had now been absent a long time, and as no word had come from him many Thebans had begun to conjecture, in ignorance of the truth, what seemed to them the most appealing outcome.

On hearing about what had happened at Thebes, Alexander decided that this was not a matter that he could neglect. He had long held suspicions about Athens and was very concerned about the Theban enterprise, lest the Spartans, who already harboured rebellious intentions, together with other Peloponnesian states and the untrustworthy Aetolians, should join in the Theban uprising. So, with this in mind, he marched across Eordaea, Elimotis and the heights of Stymphaea and Paravea, taking seven days to reach Pelinna in Thessaly. From here he then entered Boeotia six days later, so that the Thebans were not even aware that he had passed through the Gates until he reached Onchestus, accompanied by his whole army. At this point, those who had led the revolt maintained that it was Antipater's army which had arrived from Macedonia. They stood by their claim that Alexander was dead and became angry at anyone who reported that Alexander himself was approaching, suggesting that it was actually a different Alexander, the son of Aeropus, who had come.

On the following day Alexander left Onchestus and advanced towards Thebes as far as the enclosure of Iolaus. Here he encamped, allowing the Thebans three days to change their minds and send an embassy to him. However, far from giving any sign that they were about to propose a reconciliation, the cavalry actually charged out of the city against the camp, along with several of the light infantry, and discharged missiles at the advance guard, killing a few of the Macedonians. Alexander then dispatched some of his own light infantry and archers to repel the assault, and they managed this without difficulty, even though the Thebans were already close to the camp. The next day Alexander moved his whole army round to the gates which led to Eleutherae and Attica, but still held back from attacking the fortifications. Instead he set up camp a short distance from the Cadmeia, close enough to be of assistance to those Macedonians who were occupying it. However, the Thebans were guarding the Cadmeia, which they had fortified with a double stockade, so no external help could be given to those cut off within, while those within were also unable to venture out and harm the Thebans when they attacked the enemy outside. Nevertheless, Alexander, still wishing to come to the Thebans in friendship rather than in battle, waited where he was. Given the situation, those of the Thebans with the common interest in mind were eager to go out to Alexander and ask him to forgive the majority of the Thebans for the revolt; but the exiles, along with those who had summoned them, did not think it fitting to gain favour from Alexander, especially as some of them were officers of the Boeotian Confederacy. In every way they incited the people to war. Yet, even so, Alexander would not attack the city.

Now Ptolemy, the son of Lagus, claims that Perdiccas, the commander of the camp's guard, who was stationed near the enemy's stockade along with his own forces, did not wait for Alexander's signal for battle. He took it upon himself to launch the assault upon the stockade and, having torn this apart, attacked the Thebans' advance guard. Amyntas, the son of Andromenes, being part of the same unit as Perdiccas, followed him into the attack with his own troops as soon as he saw that Perdiccas had breached the stockade. When Alexander saw this happening, he led out the rest of the army, not wishing to see his men stranded and at risk from the Thebans. He signalled to the archers and the Agrianes to run out into the stockade, while he held back his personal Guard and other Guards outside.

Then Perdiccas himself was wounded and fell on the spot, as he tried to force an entry into the second stockade. He was carried back to the camp in a severe condition and it was only with difficulty that he survived the wound. Meanwhile his men joined Alexander's archers to cut the Thebans off on the sunken road which leads down to the Heracleum, and they then pursued the Thebans as they retreated towards it. Suddenly though, the Thebans turned around with a cry, and it was the Macedonians who now fled. Eurybotas the Cretan, commander of the archers, fell, along with about seventy of his men, while the remainder rushed back towards the Macedonian lines and the king's Guards.

Meanwhile, having watched his own men fleeing with the Thebans in disordered pursuit, Alexander launched an attack with a closely ordered phalanx, driving the Thebans back inside the gates. So panicked was the Theban withdrawal that they could not even shut the gates in time as they were driven back through them. This meant that those Macedonians who had been in closest pursuit actually passed with them inside the fortifications, which were now deserted, due to the large numbers of advance posts. Moving into the Cadmeia by way of the Ampheum, the Macedonians coming from this side, along with those who had been occupying the Cadmeia, now advanced into the city itself. Those troops outside now scaled the walls, already held by those who had rushed in with the retreating Thebans, and charged into the market place.

For a short time, the Theban forces near the Ampheum stood firm, but with the Macedonians hard upon them from all sides and Alexander making his presence felt all over the city, the Theban cavalry stormed through the city and charged out into the open countryside, while the infantry fought for their survival, each man for himself. No longer defended, the Thebans were slaughtered without restraint, not so much by the Macedonians, as by the Phocians, Plataeans and other Boeotians. Some were attacked in their homes as they returned there to defend them; others as suppliants in the temples; nor were the women and children spared.

The extent of the suffering endured by these Greeks, given the size of the captured city, the severity of the action and, not least, how unexpected it was both to victims and perpetrators, was just as shocking to the rest of Greece as it was to those who had been involved in it. The Athenians' Sicilian disaster had been no less catastrophic in terms of numbers of casualties. Yet, that army was slaughtered far from home, an army made up of many more allies than citizens; while the Athenians were left with their city, which they were able to defend for some time, fighting a war against the Spartans and their allies, and Persia. For these reasons that event had not been experienced as such a crushing tragedy by the Athenians, nor was the rest of Greece as horrified by their suffering. Likewise, the Athenian defeat at Aegospotami happened at sea and, even though the city was humiliated by having its Long Walls destroyed, surrendering most of its fleet and being deprived of its colonies, the structure of its government was maintained and it was not long before it had regained its former power. They had rebuilt their Long Walls, regained their sea-power, and been instrumental in delivering from the gravest danger those very Spartans whom they had earlier feared so much, and who had come so close to destroying their city. Again, with the Spartan defeat at Leuctra and Mantinea, it was the unexpectedness of the disaster that had shocked the Spartans, rather than the number of fatalities; while it was the curious spectacle of Epaminondas' Boeotian and Arcadian forces attacking Sparta, rather than the severity of the danger, which had struck such terror into the hearts of the Spartans and their allies. Then there was the capture of Plataea, which had no very grave consequences; few were taken prisoner, because the majority had already fled to Athens long before. As for the Fall of Melos and Scione, mere island fortresses, the Greeks as a whole were more disgusted at the perpetrators than surprised by the event.

The case with Thebes, however, was very different: the suddenness of the unplanned revolt; the capture accomplished so swiftly and easily by the victors; the terrible massacre, such as does indeed occur when there is long-standing animosity between kindred tribes; the entire enslavement of a city whose military power and reputation were among the most formidable in Greece – all of these things were attributed, naturally, to divine wrath. It was said that Thebes had finally paid the penalty for its betrayal of the Greeks in the Persian war; for its capture and complete enslavement of Plataea during the truce; for the slaughter of those who had surrendered to the Spartans, which was a Theban, not a Greek, action; for the devastation wrought on the countryside, in which the Greeks had swept aside the danger which faced them as they met the Persians in battle; and, finally, for voting for the destruction of Athens, when only its enslavement was proposed by Spartan alliance. It was said that God* had given many signs of the impending disaster. At the time these had been ignored; but later when they were recalled

---

* On occasion ancient authors refer to 'God', as opposed to 'the gods'. This is, however, just another way of talking about divine power and does not mean that they are moving away from polytheism.

people had come to believe that these had long foretold what had now happened.

Alexander appointed the allies who had taken part in the battle to settle affairs at Thebes. Their decision was to keep the Cadmeia, but raze the city to the ground; to divide all the land except for its holy sites amongst the allies; and to enslave the women, the children and all the Theban survivors, apart from the priests, priestesses and anyone who had been a friend of Philip or Alexander, or a patron of Macedonians. It is reported that Alexander's reverence for Pindar made him decide to preserve the house of the poet, along with his descendants. As well as all this, the allies resolved to rebuild and fortify Orchomenus and Plataea.

When news of what had happened to Thebes was relayed to the rest of Greece, the Arcadians who had left their homes to bring help to the Thebans condemned to death those who had prevailed upon them to do this, whereas the Eleans, whose relationship with Alexander was good, allowed their own exiles to return. The Aetolians sent representatives from every tribe to ask for forgiveness, claiming that they had only joined the revolt in response to the news from Thebes. As for the Athenians, they were celebrating the Great Mysteries* when some of the Thebans arrived, straight from the battle. In a state of shock, they abandoned the Mysteries and started to transfer property from the countryside into the city. The people, meanwhile, gathered in the Assembly and voted for a motion from Demades to send ten ambassadors to Alexander, selected from the Athenians known to be on the best terms with Alexander. They would bring a somewhat delayed message to Alexander that the city of Athens congratulated him on his safe return from the Illyrians and Triballians, and on his punishment of the Theban revolt. Although the tone of Alexander's response to the embassy was friendly, he wrote a letter to the Athenians demanding that the associates of Demosthenes and Lycurgus, together with Hypereides, Polyeuctas, Chares, Charidemus,

---

* Religious celebrations performed in honour of Demeter at Eleusis around September/October.

Ephialtes, Diotimus and Moerocles be handed over to him. These were the men whom Alexander deemed responsible for the city's misfortune at Chaeronea and for offences against Philip and against himself, after Philip's death. Instead of handing over the men, however, the Athenians sent yet another embassy to Alexander, this time begging him to set aside his anger against the men, and Alexander did then do so, perhaps out of respect for the city, or perhaps because he was eager to embark on his Asian expedition and wished to leave no causes for concern behind him among the Greeks. However, out of all the men whose surrender he had been refused, he did order that Charidemus be sent into exile, and the latter then fled to King Darius in Asia. (Arrian)

In the previous year a congress of the Greek states had been held at the Isthmus of Corinth: here a vote had been passed that the states should join forces with Alexander in invading Persia and that he should be commander-in-chief of the expedition. Many of the Greek statesmen and philosophers visited him to offer their congratulations, and he hoped that Diogenes of Sinope, who was at that time living in Corinth, would do the same. However, since he paid no attention whatever to Alexander, but continued to live at leisure in the suburb of Corinth which was known as Craneion, Alexander went in person to see him and found him basking at full length in the sun. When he saw so many people approaching him, Diogenes raised himself a little on his elbow and fixed his gaze upon Alexander. The king greeted him and inquired whether he could do anything for him. 'Yes,' replied the philosopher, 'you can stand a little to one side out of my sun.' Alexander is said to have been greatly impressed by this answer and full of admiration for the hauteur and independence of mind of a man who could look down on him with such condescension. So much so that he remarked to his followers, who were laughing and mocking the philosopher as they went away, 'You may say what you like, but if I were not Alexander, I would be Diogenes.'

Next he visited Delphi, because he wished to consult the oracle of Apollo about the expedition against the Persians. It so happened that he arrived on one of those days which are called inauspicious, when it is forbidden for the oracle to deliver a reply. In spite of this he sent for the prophetess, and when she refused to officiate and explained that the law forbade her to do so, he went up himself and tried to drag her by force to the shrine. At last, as if overcome by his persistence, she exclaimed, 'You are invincible, my son!' and when Alexander heard this, he declared that he wanted no other prophecy, but had obtained from her the oracle he was seeking. When the time came for him to set out, many other prodigies attended the departure of the army: among these was the phenomenon of the statue of Orpheus which was made of cypress wood and was observed to be covered with sweat. Everyone who saw it was alarmed at this omen, but Aristander urged the king to take courage, for this portent signified that Alexander was destined to perform deeds which would live in song and story and would cause poets and musicians much toil and sweat to celebrate them. (Plutarch)

3. THE PERSIAN CAMPAIGN (1) – FROM THE HELLESPONT TO GORDIUM

In May 334 Alexander sets off for the Persian empire. After crossing the Hellespont he visits the grave of Achilles at Troy and then goes on to win a difficult but decisive victory at Granicus. While many of the cities in Asia Minor then cede to Alexander, some, such as Miletus and Halicarnassus, remain loyal to the Persians and have to be taken by force.

As for the size of his army, the lowest estimate puts its strength at 30,000 infantry and 4,000 cavalry and the highest 43,000 infantry and 4,000 cavalry. According to Aristobulus the money available for the army's supplies amounted to no more than seventy talents, Douris says that there were supplies for only thirty days, and Onesicritus that Alexander was already 200 talents in debt. Yet although he set out with such slender resources, he would not go aboard his ship until he had discovered the circumstances of all his companions and had assigned an estate to one, a village to another, or the revenues of some port or community to a third. When he had shared out or signed away almost all the property of the crown, Perdiccas asked him, 'But your majesty, what are you leaving for yourself?' 'My hopes!' replied Alexander. 'Very well, then,' answered Perdiccas, 'those who serve with you will share those too.' With this, he declined to accept the prize which had been allotted to him, and several of Alexander's other friends did the same. However, those who accepted or requested rewards were lavishly provided for, so that in the end Alexander distributed among them most of what he possessed in Macedonia. These were his preparations and this was the adventurous spirit in which he crossed the Hellespont.

Once arrived in Asia, he went up to Troy, sacrificed to Athena and poured libations to the heroes of the Greek army. He anointed with oil the column which marks the grave of Achilles, ran a race by it naked with his companions, as the custom is, and then crowned it with a wreath: he also remarked that Achilles was happy in having found a faithful friend while he lived and a great poet to sing of his deeds after his death. While he was walking about the city and looking at its ancient remains, somebody asked him whether he wished to see the lyre which had once belonged to Paris. 'I think nothing of that lyre,' he said, 'but I wish I could see Achilles' lyre, which he played when he sang of the glorious deeds of brave men.'

Meanwhile Darius' generals had gathered a large army and posted it at the crossing of the river Granicus, so that Alexander was obliged to fight at the very gates of Asia, if he was to enter and conquer it. Most of the Macedonian officers were alarmed at the depth of the river and at the rough and uneven slopes of the banks on the opposite side, up which they would have to scramble in the face of the enemy. There were others too who thought that Alexander ought to observe the Macedonian tradition concerning the time of year, according to which the kings of Macedonia never made war during the month of Daesius.* Alexander swept aside these scruples by giving orders that the month should be called a second Artemisius. And when Parmenion advised him against risking the crossing at such a late hour of the day, Alexander declared that the Hellespont would blush for shame if, once he had crossed it, he should shrink back from the Granicus; then he immediately plunged into the stream with thirteen squadrons of cavalry. It seemed the act of a desperate madman rather than of a prudent commander to charge into a swiftly flowing river, which swept men off their feet and surged about them, and then to advance through a hail of missiles towards a steep bank which was strongly defended by infantry and cavalry. But in spite of this he pressed forward and

* May–June: this was the time for the gathering of the harvest.

with a tremendous effort gained the opposite bank, which was a wet treacherous slope covered with mud. There he was immediately forced to engage the enemy in a confused hand-to-hand struggle, before the troops who were crossing behind him could be organized into any formation. The moment his men set foot on land, the enemy attacked them with loud shouts, matching horse against horse, thrusting with their lances and fighting with the sword when their lances broke. Many of them charged against Alexander himself, for he was easily recognizable by his shield and by the tall white plume which was fixed upon either side of his helmet. The joint of his breastplate was pierced by a javelin, but the blade did not penetrate the flesh. Rhoesaces and Spithridates, two of the Persian commanders, then rode at him; he evaded the charge of the one and struck Rhoesaces, who wore a breastplate, with his spear, but the shaft of the weapon snapped, whereupon he fought with his sword. While he was engaged with Rhoesaces, Spithridates rode up on the other side, and rising in his stirrups brought down a barbarian battleaxe with all his strength upon Alexander's head. The stroke split the crest of his helmet, sheared away one of his plumes, and all but cleft the headpiece, in fact the edge of the axe penetrated it and grazed the hair on the top of Alexander's head. But just as Spithridates raised his arm for another blow, 'Black' Cleitus, as he was called, struck first and ran him through with a spear, and at the same moment Rhoesaces was cut down by Alexander's sword.

While Alexander's cavalry was engaged in this furious and dangerous action, the Macedonian phalanx crossed the river and the infantry of both sides joined battle. The Persians offered little resistance, but quickly broke and fled, and it was only the Greek mercenaries who held their ground. They rallied together, made a stand on the crest of a hill and sent a message to Alexander asking for quarter. In this instance he allowed himself to be guided by passion rather than by reason, led a charge against them and lost his horse (not Bucephalus on this occasion), which was pierced through the ribs by a sword-thrust. It was in this part of the field that the Macedonians suffered greater losses in killed and wounded than in all the rest of the battle, since they were fighting at close quarters with men who were expert soldiers and had been rendered desperate.

The Persians are said to have lost 20,000 infantry and 2,500 cavalry. (Plutarch)

Of the Macedonians, around twenty-five Companions died in the first assault. Bronze statues of these men have been erected at Dium. At the order of Alexander, these were sculpted by Lysippus, the only sculptor chosen to make a statue of Alexander. Over sixty other cavalry perished, along with about thirty infantry. The next day Alexander buried them with their arms and other finery, while also exempting their parents and children from local taxes and any type of personal service or tax payable on individual property. He showed great concern for the wounded and visited each of them in person to see their wounds and enquire how their injuries had come about, giving them the chance to tell and actually boast of their actions. Then Alexander even buried the Persian commanders and the Greek mercenaries who had died fighting for the enemy. Any of the mercenaries who were taken prisoner were put in fetters and sent back to Macedonia to do hard labour, their punishment for violating the peace pact among Greeks by fighting their fellow Greeks on behalf of foreigners. He also sent 300 full suits of Persian armour back to Athens as an offering to the city's goddess, Athena. He ordered the following words to be inscribed on them: 'Alexander, son of Philip, together with all the Greeks apart from the Spartans present these tributes, taken from the foreign peoples of Asia'.

Calas was appointed to the satrapy that Arsites had held and the local people were ordered to pay the same tribute that they had previously paid to Darius. Alexander told the natives who had come down from the hills to surrender that they should return to their homes, while he also absolved the people of Zeleia from blame, in the knowledge that they had been forced into fighting on the side of the Persians. Parmenion was sent to take over Dascylium, a task easily accomplished since it had been abandoned by its guards. (Arrian)

*

This battle brought about a great and immediate change in Alexander's situation. Even the city of Sardis, which was the principal seat of Persian power on the Asiatic seaboard, at once surrendered to him and the rest of the region likewise made its submission. Only Halicarnassus and Miletus held out, and these cities were stormed and the surrounding territory subdued. (Plutarch)

Alexander defeats Miletus and Halicarnassus, and then disbands the fleet.

Taking the rest of the infantry, together with the archers, the Agrianes, the Thracian cavalry, the royal squadron of Companion cavalry and three additional squadrons, he marched against Miletus. He captured what is known as the Outer City on his approach, since its guards had left, and then set up camp, having decided to blockade the Inner City. Hegesistratus, appointed by Darius commander of the Milesian guard, had previously sent a letter to Alexander in which he surrendered Miletus, but had subsequently been emboldened by the Persians' proximity and taken it upon himself to save Miletus for the Persians. Meanwhile, Nicanor had brought the Greek fleet on in front of the Persians and reached Miletus three days before them, anchoring his 160 ships at the island of Lade, just off the coast of Miletus. The Persians were too late. When their commanders learnt that Nicanor had already arrived at Lade, they sheltered under Mount Mycale, since Alexander now occupied the island. Not only had he anchored his fleet there, but he had also brought over the Thracians and about 4,000 other mercenaries to the island.

Although the Persian fleet numbered roughly 400 ships, Parmenion urged Alexander to engage in a sea battle, expecting that the Greeks would win, but also because he had been persuaded of a victorious outcome by a divine omen – an eagle had been seen perched on the shore by the stern of Alexander's ship. If the Greeks won, he argued, it would be of great benefit to the campaign as a whole, while a defeat would not be very serious, given that the Persians were already in control at sea. He even said that he would be willing to go on board one of the ships and share in the danger in person. However, Alexander replied that Parmenion's opinion was mistaken and that his interpretation of the omen was not accurate; to lead a few ships into battle against a fleet far superior in number and to take his own inexperienced fleet up against the trained Cyprians and Phoenicians would be an act of madness. In such uncertain circumstances, he would run the risk of handing the skill and daring of his Macedonians over to the Persians. Being beaten at sea would do great damage to their reputation for preeminence in battle, while the Greeks would be roused to revolt when they learnt of the naval defeat. These were the reasons he gave to demonstrate that it was not an opportune moment to engage in a sea battle. He also had a different interpretation of the omen: while the eagle was indeed favourable to him, the fact that it had appeared perched on land led him to assume that it was actually from land that his men would conquer the Persian fleet.

Meanwhile Glaucippus, a man well-respected among the Milesians, was sent to Alexander by the people and the foreign mercenaries who had responsibility for the city. He reported that the Milesians wished to allow both Alexander and the Persians open access to the city and harbours, and requested that, on these conditions, the siege should be lifted. But Alexander told Glaucippus to go back to the city as quickly as he could and tell the Milesians to prepare to do battle at dawn. Then he himself had the siege engines positioned against the walls and brought his army close, attacking the fortifications from nearby as well as launching more long-range bombardments. They could now get through wherever a section of wall had been brought down or damaged, while the Persians from Mycale were so close that they could almost see their friends and allies under siege.

As soon as Nicanor's forces saw from Lade that Alexander's men were attacking, they sailed into the harbour of Miletus, rowing beside the land, and, anchoring their triremes close together, prow to prow, at the mouth of the harbour, where it was narrowest, they blocked off both the harbour from the Persian fleet and the Milesians from Persian assistance. At this point the Milesians and the mercenaries were already under pressure from the Macedonians on all sides. Some of them threw themselves into the sea and paddled across on their upturned shields to a little unnamed island; others got into small boats, but were caught by the triremes in the mouth of the harbour as they rushed to outrun them; while the majority were killed within the city itself.

With the city in his possession, Alexander himself now launched his troops against those who had fled to the island. He ordered his soldiers to bring ladders to the prows of the triremes, so that they would be able to disembark from the ships on to the sheer sides of the island, as if climbing on to walls. However, when he saw that the men on the island were prepared to face this danger, he took pity on them because of their manifest nobility and loyalty, and he called a truce with them, on the condition that they should fight on his side; these Greek mercenaries numbered about 300. As for the Milesians themselves, any of those who had survived the capture of the city were granted their freedom and allowed to go.

The Persians continued to launch daytime assaults against the Greek fleet from Mycale, hoping to draw them out into a sea battle. At night however they were not anchored in comfort at Mycale, because they had to get water from the mouth of the Maeander, which was a long way away. Meanwhile Alexander guarded the harbour at Miletus with his fleet to prevent the Persians from forcing their way in; but he also sent Philotas, leading the cavalry and three battalions of infantry, to Mycale with orders to hinder the Persians from disembarking from their ships. As a result the Persians, who were effectively besieged within their ships without water and other provisions, sailed off to Samos, where they replenished their stocks and again set sail for Miletus.

They positioned the majority of the fleet outside the harbour, trying to draw the Macedonians out into the open sea; but they also sailed five of their vessels into the harbour between Lade and the camp, in the hope of capturing Alexander's ships empty. According to information they had received, most of the sailors from those ships had scattered, some to collect wood, some to gather provisions, while others had been instructed to go foraging. But, even though a number of sailors were not on board their vessels, Alexander was able to man ten ships with those men still present as soon as he saw the five Persian ships sailing towards him, and he sent these out against the enemy fleet at full speed, with orders to strike them head-on. Thus the Persians in the five ships saw that, contrary to their expectations, the Macedonians were making their way towards them, and they turned right around to go back to the rest of their fleet. In the retreat one of them, an Iassian craft which could not sail fast, was captured along with its crew, while the four other ships got away and escaped back to their own triremes. The Persians thus sailed away from Miletus with nothing achieved.

Alexander now decided to disband his fleet, both due to a lack of money and because he could see that it was not strong enough to face that of the Persians, and he did not wish to take risks with even a part of his forces. He also realized that he no longer needed a fleet since he already held that part of Asia with his army: capturing the coastal towns would enable him to destroy the Persian fleet, for it would mean that the Persians had no cities from which to man their ships, nor any port in Asia available for their use. This, then, was how the omen of the eagle was to be interpreted: he would conquer the ships from the land.

Once these matters were settled he marched on to Caria, following reports that a large Persian and foreign force had gathered at Halicarnassus. As he marched he took control of all the cities that lay between Miletus and Halicarnassus finally encamping near Halicarnassus, five stades away at most, in readiness of a lengthy siege. Its natural setting gave it some degree of security; but also, Memnon had long ago taken it upon himself, on his appointment by Darius as commander of lower Asia and of the entire fleet, to furnish the city with anything that it appeared to lack in terms of protection. A large force of foreign mercenaries, together with many Persians, had been left in the city, while triremes were guarding its harbour, able to provide naval assistance if the need arose.

On the first day, as Alexander approached the walls at the

gates leading to Mylasa, the soldiers in the town launched a short attack and fired missiles at long range. He responded with a counter-attack which easily drove the attackers back, and blockaded them within the city. A few days later, Alexander made his way around the city to the area which faces towards Myndus, taking his Guards, the Companion cavalry, the infantry division of Amyntas, Perdiccas and Meleager, the archers and the Agrianes. He wanted to assess the strength of the fortifications there, hoping that he would be able to launch an unexpected raid on Myndus, the capture of which would be a great help in the siege of Halicarnassus. Some of the people in Myndus had, in fact, offered to surrender to him, as long as he made a stealthy night-time attack. According to this arrangement, he approached the fortifications around midnight. Yet no surrender came from those within. Now he did not have siege engines and ladders with him, because he had been prepared for a treacherous surrender and not for a siege, so he ordered the Macedonian phalanx to bring down the wall. Although they did destroy one tower, the wall remained standing, and a strong defence from those within the city, together with the large number of reinforcements who had already come in by sea from Halicarnassus, prevented Alexander from achieving the sudden and speedy capture of Myndus. So, without having accomplished what he had set out to do, Alexander turned back, and once again directed his attention to the siege of Halicarnassus.

The first thing he did was to fill in the moat which had been dug around the city, which was about 45 feet wide and 23 feet deep. This was done so that it would be easier to put into place the towers from which he intended to bombard those who were defending the fortifications as well as the other siege engines with which he was planning to bring down the walls themselves. Filling the moat presented no difficulty, and the towers were positioned straight away. Then, during the night, a group rushed out of Halicarnassus to burn the towers and all the siege engines which were either already in place or close at hand. However, the Macedonian guards, together with those who had come to help after waking up during the assault, easily drove the attackers back again within their walls. There were 170 fatalities

among the attackers, including Neoptolemus, son of Arrabaeus,
the brother of Amyntas, one of those who had deserted to
Darius. Among Alexander's troops there were about sixteen
deaths. Nevertheless, around 300 men were injured because the
night-time attack had left them without adequate protection
against wounds.

Not many days later, two of the heavily armed soldiers from
Perdiccas' contingent were boasting about themselves and their
achievements as they drank together in their tent. A desire to
prove themselves then took hold of them, intensified by the
wine, so that they took up their arms and attacked the wall on
the high ground which faces in the direction of Mylasa. Their
aim was really only to show off their own prowess, rather than
to engage with the enemy in risky combat; but when some of
the men in the city caught sight of them, they rushed out at these
two lone soldiers as they made their irrational assault on the
wall. However, the men killed those who came close and also
launched missiles at the more distant troops, even though they
were outnumbered and the harsh terrain meant that the assault
and missiles of the Halicarnassians were coming from above
them. Meanwhile some more of Perdiccas' soldiers rushed out,
and more men also came out of the city as well, and a fierce battle
broke out by the wall. Once again, those who had launched the
assault were driven back within the gates by the Macedonians
and the city came close to being taken. Indeed, the walls were
without sufficient protection during that period, while two
towers, along with the section in between, had collapsed, which
would have allowed the Macedonians easy access to the city, if
they had launched a unified attack. Moreover, a third tower
had also been damaged and would easily have come down if
they had put mines under it. But inside the town they had been
quick to erect a crescent-shaped brick wall behind the damaged
wall, a task achieved easily as there were many people to help.

On the next day, Alexander brought his siege engines up to
this wall, and those within the town immediately sent out a
party to burn down the engines. Some part of the wicker fences
near the fortifications, together with one wooden tower, was
burnt down; but Philotas' and Hellanicus' soldiers saved the

rest of the weapons, whose protection they had been entrusted with. Then, seeing Alexander taking part in the skirmish, most of the attackers fled back inside the walls, discarding the torches that they had brought out for the raid and throwing down their arms. Even so, those within the town still had the upper hand due to their position on high ground. This meant that they could fire missiles not only straight ahead at the foremost siege engines, but also, from the towers which remained on either side of the breached wall and on the flanks and almost on the rear of the troops as they approached the newly built barrier.

When, a few days later, Alexander took charge of operations in person and again led his siege engines up to the inner brick wall, the men inside the city counter-attacked in full force. Some launched their assault from near the breach in the wall, where Alexander himself was positioned; some from near the Triple Gate, where the Macedonians were least expecting an attack; others threw torches, along with anything else which might set them alight and spread the flames, at the siege engines. They encountered a powerful offensive from Alexander's troops. Hurling huge stones and firing missiles from the siege engines on the towers, the latter repelled the enemy without difficulty and drove them back into the city. The daring counter-attack had been attempted with a large number of troops, and the enemy's losses were consequently great: some men perished in close combat with the Macedonians; others around the breach in the wall, since their numbers could not pass through the narrow gap, nor climb over the broken bits of wall without difficulty. Those who were attacking near the Triple Gate were met by Ptolemy, the commander of the Royal Guards, together with the battalions of Addaeus and Timander and some of the light infantry, who easily drove back the men who had come out of the city. As they retreated, these men also met with disaster: the narrow bridge over which they were making their escape in great numbers collapsed into the moat. Some were trampled to death by their comrades, while others were shot down from above by the Macedonians. However, the worst slaughter took place around the gates themselves, which were closed too early in panic, out of fear that the Macedonian aggressors might enter along with those who were fleeing. Thus the defenders shut out many of their comrades, who were then slaughtered by the Macedonians right by the walls. At this point the city was close to being captured. However, Alexander called back the army, still wishing to save Halicarnassus, as long as the citizens were prepared to surrender amicably. The death toll for those in the city was around 1,000, while forty of Alexander's men died, including Ptolemy, commander of the Royal Guards, Clearchus, who led the archers, Addaeus, who led a force of 1,000, and various other important Macedonians.

At this, the Persian commanders Orontobates and Memnon met and decided that, given the current situation, they would not be able to hold out against the siege for much longer; for they could see that part of the wall had already collapsed, while another section was damaged, and that they had lost many soldiers in the sallies, some dead, others wounded and unfit to fight. With all of this in mind, around the second watch of the night, they set fire to the wooden tower that they had erected themselves as a defence against the enemy siege engines, and to the shelters where they had stored their weapons. They also set alight the houses near the walls, while the flames from the armouries and tower, which had become a great conflagration, were carried by the wind towards other houses, which then caught fire as well. The men themselves retreated, either to the island citadel or to the heights called Salmakis. As soon as reports of the fire were brought to Alexander by Halicarnassian deserters, and he saw it with his own eyes, he led out the Macedonians, even though it was around midnight, and gave them orders to kill those still lighting fires in the city, but to save any of the citizens of Halicarnassus found in their houses.

Dawn was already breaking and the heights occupied by the Persians and the mercenaries became visible. Alexander decided against besieging them, realizing that their vantage position would make this a long and difficult endeavour, and that it would not be of much help to him, since he had already taken the city. So, after burying those who had perished during the night, he ordered the soldiers who looked after the siege engines to take them to Tralles, before razing the city to the ground.

Leaving behind 3,000 mercenary foot soldiers, together with 200 cavalry, to guard the city and the rest of Caria under the command of Ptolemy, he then set off for Phrygia.

He appointed Ada as satrap for the whole of Caria. She was the daughter of Hecatomnus and wife of Hidrieus, who, in line with Carian customs, had been both her brother and her husband. Ever since the rule of Semiramis, it had been normal in Asia for women to rule over men and, at the time of his death, Hidrieus had handed over his duties to Ada. Nevertheless, Pixodarus ousted her from power and assumed control himself and, when he died, Orontobates, his brother-in-law, was sent by the king to rule over the Carians. Ada meanwhile held only Alinda, one of Caria's strongholds. When Alexander entered Caria, she went out to meet him, ceding Alinda to him and offering to make him her adopted son. Alexander then gave Alinda back to her without turning down the proposed adoption and, when he captured Halicarnassus and took over the rest of Caria, he made her the ruler of the entire realm.

Some of Alexander's Macedonian troops had married just before this campaign. Realizing that it would not be right to neglect them, he sent them back from Caria to spend the winter in Macedonia with their wives, putting Ptolemy, son of Seleucus and one of the Royal Guard, along with the commanders Coenus, son of Polemocrates, and Meleager, son of Neopto-lemus, who had themselves recently married, in charge of them. He told them that when it was time for them to return and to bring back their men, they should gather together as great a number of cavalry and foot soldiers as possible. It was this action, as much as any other, which gave Alexander his good reputation among the Macedonians. (Arrian)

At this point Alexander hesitated as to what his next step should be. Time and again he was impelled to seek out Darius and risk everything upon the issue of a single battle, and then as often he would decide that he must build up his strength by securing the coastal region and its resources and training his army, and only then strike inland against the king. It is said that there was a spring near the city of Xanthus, in the province of Lycia, which at this moment overflowed and cast up from its depths a bronze tablet: this was inscribed with ancient characters which foretold that the empire of the Persians would be destroyed by the Greeks. Alexander was encouraged by this prophecy and pressed on to clear the coast of Asia Minor as far as Cilicia and Phoenicia. His advance through Pamphylia inspired various historians to compose a highly wrought and extravagant description of his progress. They imply that through some extraordinary stroke of providence their tide receded to make way for him, although at other times it came flooding in strongly from the open sea, so that the beach of small rocks which lies directly under the steep and broken face of the cliffs was hardly ever left uncovered. Menander alludes to this prodigy in one of his comedies, where he says:

> Like Alexander, if I want to meet
> A man, he's there before me in the street,
> And if I am obliged to cross the sea,
> The waves at once will make a path for me.

Alexander makes no mention in his letters of any such miracle, but says that he started from Phaselis in Lycia, and marched through Pamphylia by the pass known as *Klimax*, or The Ladder. It as for this reason that he spent several days in Phaselis, where he noticed in the market-place a statue which had been erected in honour of Theodectas, a former citizen of the place. One evening after dinner when he had drunk well, he had the impulse to pay a convivial tribute to his association with Aristotle and with philosophy, and so he led a band of revellers to the statue and crowned it with a garland.

Next he marched into Pisidia where he subdued any resistance which he encountered, and then made himself master of Phrygia. (Plutarch)

Alexander then moves on to Gordium.

When Alexander arrived in Gordium, he was seized by the desire to go up to the acropolis, to the palace of Gordius and his son

Midas, in order to see Gordius' wagon and the knot in the wagon's yoke. This wagon was the subject of a legend famous among the people of the region: Gordius was said to have been a poor man of ancient Phrygian stock who worked his small patch of land and had just two yoke of oxen – one he used for ploughing, the other to drive his oxen. One day, while he was ploughing, an eagle landed on the yoke and remained perched there until the oxen were untied. Astonished by the sight, Gordius went to consult the Telmissian seers to ask about this omen; for the Telmissian people were very knowledgeable in matters of divine interpretation and even the women and children had inherited this prophetic gift. As he approached one of the Telmissian villages, he came across a girl who was drawing water and told her about what had happened to him with the eagle. Now she was herself a seer by birth, and instructed him to go back to where he had come from and sacrifice to Zeus the King. Gordius then beseeched her to accompany him and explain how he should carry out the sacrifice. When he had performed the sacrifice as she instructed, he married her and a child was born to them, named Midas. Midas had already grown into a handsome and noble man when civil war broke out among the Phrygians. The Phrygians were told that a chariot would bring them a king who would then put a stop to the unrest. Even as they were deliberating over how to respond to this oracle, Midas arrived in the chariot, along with his mother and father, and came to a halt among their assembly. They then took the oracle to mean that this was the man whom the gods had told them would be brought by a chariot. Midas was made king and he did subsequently put an end to the unrest. He set his father's chariot on the acropolis as an offering of thanks to Zeus the King for sending the eagle.

Yet there was also another story connected with the wagon: that whoever managed to loose the knot from the wagon's yoke must rule over Asia. The knot was made from cornel bark, with its beginning and end concealed from view, and, although Alexander was at a loss as to how to untie it, he was not willing to let it remain tied in case this led to a popular uprising. Some say that he struck it with his sword and cut it, then claimed to have undone it. However, Aristobulus claims that he took out the pin from the pole – this was a peg driven all the way through the pole to hold it together – and that he then pulled the yoke from the pole. I myself cannot be certain as to how the affair of Alexander and the knot took place. Suffice to say that when he and his entourage left behind the wagon, it was as if the oracle of the loosening of the knot had been fulfilled. During the night there were even signs from heaven to this effect – thunder and lightning – and Alexander gave due sacrifice the next day to the gods whose signs had proclaimed the loosening of the knot. (Arrian)

4. THE PERSIAN CAMPAIGN (2) – FROM CAPPADOCIA TO EGYPT

Memnon, the supreme commander of the Persian forces, takes over various member cities of Alexander's Greek alliance. However, he dies suddenly, a considerable setback for the Persian king, Darius, and a boost for Alexander. Alexander then moves eastwards and, after a delay through illness at Tarsus, finally meets Darius in battle at Issus, where he wins a decisive victory, but shows clemency towards Darius' captured family. While the defeated Darius flees back towards his Persian strongholds, Alexander continues to move through the Middle East, taking severe action against any cities prepared to resist. Alexander is welcomed in Egypt and searches for his divine roots from the oracle of the god Zeus Ammon at the desert town of Siwah. It is also in Egypt that he lays the foundations of the great city of Alexandria.

After this had happened, Memnon – to whom Darius had given the command of the whole fleet together with the entire coastline, so as to divert the war into Macedonia and Greece – captured Chios, which was surrendered through treachery. From there he sailed to Lesbos and, although the citizens of Mytilene would not join him, he won over all the remaining cities of Lesbos. After taking command of them he landed at Mytilene and fenced off the city with a double stockade which went up from the sea on one side of the island right to the other side. Then, by setting up five encampments, he easily took control of the land. While some of his ships guarded the harbour, he sent others to Sigrium, the promontory of Lesbos, where the merchants' ships from Chios, Geraistus and Malea usually land. This is how he kept the coastline secure, preventing any help from coming to the people of Mytilene by sea.

However, in the middle of all this, he died from an illness, an event which harmed the Persian king's cause more than any other event at that time. (Arrian)

Darius was duly distressed by the news of Memnon's death. Abandoning hope of any other option, he decided to take to the field in person; for, in fact, he was critical of all the actions of his generals, believing that most lacked military precision and all of them good luck. So he encamped at Babylon and, to enable his forces to start the war with increased confidence, he put on a public display of his entire strength. He encircled with a ditch an area that could hold 10,000 armed soldiers and began a numerical review using Xerxes' method. From sunrise to night-fall columns of armed men entered the enclosure in a prescribed order and, on being discharged from it, took up a position on the Mesopotamian plains, a host of cavalrymen and foot soldiers almost beyond number and creating the impression of being more than they really were. There were 100,000 Persians, including 30,000 cavalry, while the Medes numbered 10,000 cavalry and 50,000 infantry. There were 2,000 Barcanian cavalry armed with double-headed axes and small shields (closer in appearance to the *cetra** than anything else); and they were followed by 10,000 Barcanian infantry who were similarly armed. The Armenians had sent 40,000 infantry along with 7,000 cavalry. The Hyrcanians had mustered a total of 6,000 horsemen of excellent quality – by the standards of those peoples, that is – reinforced with 1,000 Tapurian cavalry. The Derbices had 40,000 infantrymen under arms, most of them equipped with bronze- or iron-tipped lances, but a few had just lances of wood hardened by fire. Along with these came 2,000 cavalrymen of the same race. From the Caspian Sea had come 8,000 foot and 200 horse and, with them, other lesser-known tribes who had mustered 2,000 infantry and twice as many

* Small Spanish shield.

cavalry. These forces were supplemented by 30,000 Greek mercenaries, a superb group of young soldiers. As for Bactrians, Sogdians, Indians and others living on the Red Sea (some of whose names were unknown even to Darius), the hurried mobilization precluded their being summoned.

But the one thing Darius did not lack was military numbers. The sight of this assembly filled him with joy, and his courtiers further inflated his expectations with their usual idle flattery. He turned to the Athenian Charidemus, who was an experienced soldier with a grudge against Alexander because of his exile (it was on Alexander's command that he had been expelled from Athens), and he proceeded to ask whether, in his opinion, he was well enough equipped to crush his enemy. With no thought for his own circumstances and the vanity of royalty, Charidemus answered, 'Perhaps you do not want to be told the truth and yet, if I do not tell it now, it will serve no purpose to admit it at another time. This magnificent army, this conglomeration of so many nations drawn from their homes all over the East, can strike terror into your neighbours. It gleams with purple and gold; it is resplendent with armour and an opulence so great that those who have not witnessed it simply cannot conceive of it. The Macedonian line is certainly coarse and inelegant, but it protects behind its shields and lances immovable wedges of tough, densely packed soldiers. The Macedonians call it a phalanx, an infantry column that holds its ground. They stand man next to man, arms interlocked with arms. They wait eagerly for their commander's signal, and they are trained to follow the standards and not break ranks. To a man they obey their orders. Standing ground, encircling manoeuvres, running to the wings, changing formation – the common soldier is no less skilled at all this than the officer. And don't think that what motivates them is the desire for gold and silver; until now such strict discipline has been due to poverty's schooling. When they are tired, the earth is their bed; they are satisfied with food they can prepare while they work; their sleeping time is of shorter duration than the darkness. And now I suppose cavalry from Thessaly, Acarnania, Aetolia – troops that are unbeaten in war – are going to be driven off by slings and by lances hardened in fire! What you need is strength like theirs. You must look for help in the land that produced those men – send off that silver and gold of yours to hire *soldiers*.'

Darius was of a mild and placid disposition, but even natural inclinations are generally corrupted by fortune. Unable to take the truth, he had Charidemus dragged off to execution, guest and suppliant though he was, and at a time when he was making very useful recommendations. Even in these circumstances, Charidemus did not forget that he was a free man, 'I have the avenger of my death ready at hand,' he declared. 'You will pay the penalty for rejecting my advice, and pay it to the very man against whom it was given. As for you, so suddenly transformed by your unlimited power, you shall be an example to posterity of how men can forget even their natural inclinations when they have surrendered themselves to fortune.' He was shouting this aloud when those ordered to do so slit his throat. Then, all too late, the king experienced a change of heart and, admitting the truth of Charidemus' words, ordered his burial. (Curtius)

Meanwhile Alexander presses on into Cilicia and enters the Town of Tarsus, deserted by the Persian forces before his arrival.

Alexander now fell ill; according to Aristobulus, from exhaustion, though others say that he had dived into the river Cydnus to go swimming, longing for the water, worn out and sweating. The Cydnus runs through the middle of the city of Tarsus and is cold and clear, because its springs rise from Mount Tarsus and flow through the open country. This led to Alexander succumbing to convulsions, a strong fever and relentless insomnia. While all the other doctors believed that he could not survive the illness, Philip of Acarnia, a doctor who looked after Alexander, wanted to administer a purgative draught. Alexander not only trusted Philip in medical matters, but also respected him in military terms, so he instructed him to proceed with the purgative. However, jut as he was preparing the medicine, a letter from Parmenion was handed to Alexander, in which he warned him to be on his guard against Philip, since Parmenion had heard that Darius had bribed him to poison Alexander. Alexander read the letter and, while he still held it in his hand, took hold of the cup which contained the concoction, before giving the letter to Philip. At the very same moment that Philip read the words of Parmenion, Alexander drank. It was immediately obvious that Philip had done nothing wrong with the draught. Far from being shocked by the letter, he simply encouraged Alexander to carry on with the instructions he had written. He insisted that obeying his instructions would lead to recovery. The illness was alleviated by the purgative, while Alexander also proved his firm friendship to Philip, his unwavering trust in his comrades, and his strength, even in the face of death. (Arrian)

There was at this time in Darius' army, a man named Amyntas, a refugee from Macedonia who was acquainted with Alexander's character. When he learned that Darius was eager to advance and attack Alexander as he marched through the mountain passes, he begged the Persian king to remain where he was in the flat open plains, where his immense numbers would have the advantage in fighting the small Macedonian army. Darius said that he was afraid the enemy might run away before he could come to grips with them, and that Alexander might thus escape him, to which Amyntas retorted, 'Your majesty need have no fears on that score. Alexander will march against you, in fact he is probably on his way now.' Darius refused to listen to Amyntas' advice, but broke camp and advanced into Cilicia, while at the same time Alexander marched against him into Syria. During the night they missed one another and both turned back. Alexander, delighted at his good fortune, hastened to catch his enemy in the narrow defile which leads into Cilicia, while Darius was no less eager to extricate his forces from the mountain passes and regain his former camping ground in the plains. He already saw the mistake he had made by advancing into country which was hemmed in by the sea on one side and the mountains on the other, and divided by the river Pinarus, which ran between them. Here the ground prevented him from using his cavalry, forced him to split up his army into small groups, and favoured his opponent's inferior numbers. Fortune certainly presented Alexander with the ideal terrain for battle, but it was his own generalship which did most to win the victory. For although he was so heavily outnumbered, he not only gave the enemy no opportunity to encircle him, but leading his own right wing in person, he managed to extend it round the enemy's left, outflanked it and, fighting in the foremost ranks, put the barbarians to flight. In this action he received a sword wound in the thigh: according to Chares this was given him by Darius, with whom he engaged in hand-to-hand combat. Alexander sent a letter to Antipater describing the battle, but made no mention in it of who had given him the wound: he said no more than that he had been stabbed in the thigh with a dagger and that the wound was not a dangerous one.

The result of this battle was a brilliant victory for Alexander. His men killed 110,000 of the enemy, but he could not catch Darius, who had got a start of half a mile or more, although he captured the king's chariots and his bow before he returned from the pursuit. He found the Macedonians busy carrying off the spoils from the enemy's camp, for this contained an immense wealth of possessions, despite the fact that the Persians had marched into battle lightly equipped and had left most of their baggage in Damascus. Darius' tent, which was full of many treasures, luxurious furniture and lavishly dressed servants, had been set aside for Alexander himself. As soon as he arrived, he unbuckled his armour and went to the bath, saying, 'Let us wash off the sweat of battle in Darius's bath.' 'No, in Alexander's bath, now,' remarked one of his companions. 'The conqueror takes over the possessions of the conquered and they should be called his.' When Alexander entered the bath-room he saw that the basins, the pitchers, the baths themselves and the caskets containing unguents were all made of gold and elaborately carved, and noticed that the whole room was marvellously fragrant with spices and perfumes, and then, passing from this into a spacious and lofty tent, he observed the magnificence of the dining couches, the tables and the banquet which had been set out for him. He turned to his companions and remarked, 'So this, it seems, is what it is to be a king.'

As he was about to sit down to supper, word was brought to him that the mother, the wife and the two unmarried daughters of Darius were among the prisoners, and that at the sight of the Persian king's bow and chariot they had beaten their breasts and cried out, since they supposed that he must be dead. When he heard this Alexander was silent for some time, for he was evidently more affected by the women's grief than by his own triumph. Then he sent Leonnatus to tell them that Darius was not dead and that they need have no fear of Alexander: he was fighting Darius for the empire of Asia, but they should be provided with everything they had been accustomed to regard as their due when Darius was king. This kindly and reassuring message for Darius' womenfolk was followed by still more generous actions. Alexander gave them leave to bury as many of the Persians as they wished, and to take from the plunder any clothes and ornaments they thought fit and use them for this purpose. He also followed them to keep the same attendants and privileges that they had previously enjoyed, and even increased their revenues. But the most honourable and truly regal service which he rendered to these chaste and noble women was to ensure that they should never hear, suspect nor have cause to fear anything which could disgrace them: they lived out of sight and earshot of the soldiers, as though they were guarded in some inviolable retreat set aside for virgin priestesses rather than in an enemy's camp. This was the more remarkable because the wife of Darius was said to have been the most beautiful princess of her time, just as Darius himself was the tallest and handsomest man in Asia, and their daughters resembled their parents.

At any rate Alexander, so it seems, thought it more worthy of a king to subdue his own passions than to conquer his enemies, and so he never came near these women, nor did he associate with any other before his marriage, with the exception only of Barsine. This woman, the widow of Memnon, the Greek mercenary commander, was captured at Damascus. She had received a Greek education, was of a gentle disposition, and could claim royal descent, since her father was Artabazus, who had married one of the Persian king's daughters. These qualities made Alexander the more willing – he was encouraged by Parmenion, so Aristobulus tells us – to form an attachment to a woman of such beauty and noble lineage. As for the other prisoners, when Alexander saw their handsome and stately appearance, he took no more notice of them than to say jokingly, 'These Persian women are a torment for our eyes.' He was determined to make such a show of his chastity and self-control as to eclipse the beauty of their appearance, and so he passed them by as if they had been so many lifeless images cut out of stone. (Plutarch)

After the battle of Issus he sent a force to Damascus and there captured the whole of the Persian army's treasure and baggage, together with their wives and children. On this occasion it was the Thessalian cavalry who obtained the richest share of the plunder. They had particularly distinguished themselves at Issus, and Alexander had deliberately sent them on this expedition to reward them for their courage, but the booty proved so inexhaustible that there was enough to make the whole army rich. It was here that the Macedonians received their first taste of gold and silver and women and of the luxury of the barbarian way of life, and henceforth, like hounds which have picked up a scent, they pressed on to track down the wealth of the Persians.

    However, this did not divert Alexander from his strategy of securing the whole of the Asiatic seaboard before striking inland. The kings of Cyprus promptly visited him to hand over the island, and the whole of Phoenicia surrendered to him except for the city of Tyre. (Plutarch)

Surpassing all other cities of Syria and Phoenicia in size and renown, Tyre seemed more likely to accept the status of ally with Alexander than subjection to him. Tyrian envoys now brought him a gift of a golden crown, and they had already shown their hospitality by conveying to him a plentiful supply of provisions from the city. Alexander gave orders that the gifts be received as a gesture of friendship, and in a warm address to the envoys he stated his wish to sacrifice to Hercules, a deity especially revered by the people of Tyre. The Macedonian kings, he told them, believed themselves descendants of the god, and furthermore he had been advised by an oracle to make this sacrifice. The envoys replied that there was a temple of Hercules outside the city in the area which they called Palaetyros, and there the king would be able to offer due sacrifice to the god. Alexander lost his temper, which he also failed to control on other occasions. 'You think nothing of this land army,' he said, 'because of your confidence in your position, living as you do on an island, but I am soon going to show you that you are really on the mainland. And you can be sure that I shall either enter your city or storm it.'

Dismissed with this message, the envoys began to advise their fellow citizens to let into the city the king who had already been given recognition by Syria and Phoenicia, but the Tyrians had sufficient confidence in their position to decide to withstand a siege. The strait separating the city from the mainland had a width of four stades. It was particularly exposed to the south-westerly wind, which rolled rapid successions of waves on to the shore from the open sea, and nothing represented a greater obstacle to a siege work – which the Macedonians were contemplating, to join island and mainland – than this wind. In fact, to construct moles here is difficult even when the sea is smooth and calm, but the south-westerly undermines the initial foundations as the sea batters them violently. No mole is strong enough to withstand the corrosive force of the waves as the water seeps through the joints in the construction and, as the wind increases, floods over the very top of the structure. Apart from this there was another difficulty no less serious: the city walls and their turrets were surrounded by especially deep water. This meant that projectiles could be directed at them only from ships and at a distance, that scaling ladders could not be set against the walls, and that any approach by foot was out of the question since the wall dropped sheer into the sea. The king had no ships, but even if he had been able to bring some up, they could have been kept at bay with missiles because of their instability in the water.

Meanwhile a trivial event boosted the confidence of the Tyrians. A delegation of Carthaginians had arrived at that time to celebrate an annual religious festival in accordance with their tradition (Carthage having been founded by Tyre, which was always honoured as its parent-city). The Carthaginians began to encourage the Tyrians to face the siege with confidence; help, they said, would soon be coming from Carthage (in those days the seas were to a large extent dominated by Carthaginian fleets). The people of Tyre accordingly decided on war. They deployed their artillery along the walls and turrets, distributed weapons to the younger men, and allocated the city's generous resources of craftsmen to workshops. Tyre re-echoed with the noise of war preparations. Iron 'hands', called 'harpagones', for throwing on the enemy siege works, were manufactured in advance, along with 'crows' and other devices used for defending cities. It is said that when the metal that was to be forged had been set in the furnaces and the bellow-blasts were fanning the fire, streams of blood appeared beneath the flames, which the Tyrians interpreted as an omen unfavourable to the Macedonians. On the Macedonian side, too, while some soldiers happened to be breaking bread they noticed drops of blood oozing from it. Alexander was alarmed at this, but their most accomplished soothsayer, Aristander, claimed it would have been a bad omen for the Macedonians if the blood had run on the outside of the bread, but since it had run from the inside, it actually portended destruction for the city they had determined to besiege.

Since Alexander's navy was a long way off and he could see that a protracted siege would severely impede his other plans, he sent heralds to urge the Tyrians to accept peace terms; but the latter, violating international conventions, killed them and threw their bodies into the sea. Outraged by the disgraceful murder of his men, Alexander now resolved to lay siege to the city.

First, however, a mole had to be constructed to join the city and the mainland, and the sight of the fathomless deep filled the soldiers with despair, for it could scarcely be filled even if they had divine aid. How could rocks big enough be found, or trees tall enough? To make a mound to fill such a void they would have to denude whole regions; the strait was perpetually stormy, and the more constricted the area of its movement between the island and the mainland, the more fierce it became. But Alexander was not inexperienced in dealing with the soldier's temperament: he announced that he had seen in a dream the figure of Hercules extending his right hand to him, and himself entering Tyre as Hercules led him and opened the way. He included a reference to the murdered heralds, and the Tyrians' violation of international conventions, and added that this was the only city that had dared delay his victorious progress. Then the generals were instructed to reprove their men, and when they were all sufficiently aroused he set to work.

Large quantities of rock were available, furnished by old Tyre, while timber to construct rafts and siege towers was hauled from Mount Libanus. The structure had reached some height from the sea-bed without yet breaking the surface of the water when the Tyrians began to bring up small boats and to hurl insulting taunts at them about 'those famous warriors carrying loads on their backs like pack animals'. They would ask, too, if Alexander 'had more power than Neptune'. Their jeers actually served to fuel the soldiers' enthusiasm. Little by little the mole now began to rise above the surface and the mound's width increased as it approached the city. The Tyrians, who had hitherto failed to notice the mole's growth, now perceived its size. With their light skiffs they began to encircle the structure, which was not yet joined to the island, attacking with missiles the men standing by the work. Many were wounded without a casualty on the part of the Tyrians, who could both withdraw and bring up their boats without hindrance; and so the Macedonians were diverted from their work to protecting themselves. Furthermore, as the mole proceeded further from shore, the materials piled on it were increasingly sucked into the sea's depths. Alexander, therefore, had hides and sheets of canvas stretched before the workmen to screen them from Tyrian missiles, and he erected two turrets on the top of the mole from which weapons could be directed at approaching boats. The Tyrians, in turn, landed their boats on the coast well out of sight of their enemy, put soldiers ashore, and cut down the Macedonians who were carrying the rocks. On Mount Libanus, too, Arab peasants made an attack on the Macedonians while they were scattered, killing some thirty of them and taking a smaller number prisoner.

The incident obliged Alexander to split his forces. Not to appear to be frittering away time in besieging a single city, he gave the operation to Perdiccas and Craterus while he himself made for Arabia with a detachment of light-armed troops. Meanwhile the Tyrians took an enormous ship, loaded its stern with rocks and sand so that its prow stood high out of the water, and daubed it with bitumen and sulphur. Then they rowed out the ship, which, after its sails caught a strong wind, quickly came up to the mole. At this point the oarsmen fired the prow and then jumped into boats that had followed the ship expressly for this purpose. The vessel flared up and began to spread the blaze over a large area. Before help could be brought it engulfed the towers and other structures built on the top of the mole. The men who had jumped into the small boats also tossed firebrands and anything else that would fuel the flames on to these buildings; the topmost sections of the turrets, as well as the lower ones, had now caught fire, while the Macedonians on them were either consumed in the conflagration or else threw aside their arms and hurled themselves into the sea. Preferring to take them alive rather than kill them, the Tyrians would beat their hands with sticks and stones as they swam until they were disabled and could be safely taken on board. Nor was it just a matter of the superstructure being burned down. The same day it so happened that an especially high wind whipped up the sea from its very depths and smashed it against the mole. The joints loosened under the repeated battering of the waves, and water running between the rocks caused the work to rupture in the centre. As a result the mounds of stones supporting the earth heaped on the mole collapsed, and the whole structure crashed into the deep water, so that on his return from Arabia Alexander found scarcely a trace of his huge mole.

There followed what usually happens when things go wrong: they resorted to mutual recrimination when they might have complained with more justice about the violence of the sea. The king set to work on a fresh mole, but now he aimed it directly into the head-wind, instead of side-on to it, so that the front offered protection to the rest of the work which, as it were, sheltered behind it. Alexander also added breadth to the mound so that towers could be raised in the middle out of range of the enemy's missiles. Moreover, the Macedonians threw into the sea entire trees complete with their huge branches on which they set a load of rocks. Then they added another mass of trees to the pile and heaped earth on them; and over this they built up another layer of rocks and trees, thus forming a structure virtually bonded together into a solid whole.

The Tyrians meanwhile applied themselves energetically to any device that might impede the mole. Particularly helpful to their purpose were the swimmers who would submerge out of their enemies' sight and swim unobserved right up to the mole, where they would pull towards them with hooks the projecting branches of the trees. Often these came away, taking much of the building material into the deep water, and the swimmers then had little difficulty managing the logs and tree trunks, once the weight on them had been removed. After that the whole structure, which had been supported by the logs, followed into the deep when its base collapsed.

Alexander was dejected, undecided whether to continue or leave. At this point the fleet arrived from Cyprus, and Cleander simultaneously came with the Greek soldiers who had recently sailed to Asia. Alexander split the 190 ships into two wings: the Cypriot king, Pnytagoras, and Craterus took command of the left, and Alexander himself sailed on the right in the royal quinquereme. The Tyrians had a fleet, but they refused to risk a naval engagement, setting a mere three vessels in the Macedonians' path directly below the city walls. These Alexander rammed and sank.

The next day he brought the fleet up to the city's fortifications. At all points his artillery, especially his battering rams, shook the walls. The Tyrians hurriedly repaired the damage by setting rocks in the breaches and also started an inner wall which would give them protection should the first wall give way. But disaster was closing in on them at every point: the mole was within javelin range; Alexander's fleet was encircling their walls; they were facing disaster in a battle waged concurrently on land and sea. The Macedonians had lashed pairs of quadriremes together in such a way that the prows were locked together but the sterns were as far separated as could be managed. The space between the sterns they had filled with yardarms and stout beams bound together, with decking laid over these to form platforms for infantrymen. After equipping the quadriremes in this manner they moved them up to the city, and from there missiles could be safely discharged on the defenders because the infantrymen were protected by the prows.

At midnight Alexander ordered his fleet, equipped as described above, to encircle the walls and, as the ships closed in on the city at all points, a numbing despair descended on the Tyrians. Then, suddenly, thick clouds shrouded the sky and a layer of fog extinguished such twilight as there was. By degrees the sea began to roughen and swell; a stronger wind whipped it up into waves and the vessels started to collide with each other. The lashings keeping the quadriremes together began to snap and the platforms to shatter with a huge roar, dragging the soldiers with them into the deep. Since the vessels were lashed together, manoeuvring them in the rough water was impossible: infantrymen obstructed oarsmen in the performance of their tasks and oarsmen infantrymen. And as usually happens in such circumstances, the skilled began to obey the unskilled, with helmsmen, who customarily gave orders, now following instructions out of fear for their lives. The sea, lashed by their oars with greater determination, finally surrendered the vessels to the sailors, their rescuers, who brought them to shore, most of them as wrecks.

Thirty ambassadors from Carthage happened to arrive during this period, more to encourage the besieged than to help them – for the Carthaginians, they announced to the Tyrians, were handicapped by a war at home and were fighting not for power but simply for survival. The Syracusans were even then putting the torch to the crops in Africa, and had made camp not far from the walls of Carthage. Though frustrated in their great expectations, the Tyrians did not lose heart; instead they handed over their wives and children for evacuation to Carthage, being ready to face whatever might happen with increased fortitude if they had the most previous part of their community removed from the common peril. One of their fellow citizens had also made it known at an assembly that he had dreamed that Apollo, a deity especially revered by the Tyrians, was leaving the city, and that the mole laid in the sea by the Macedonians turned into a woodland glade. Despite the unreliability of the speaker, the Tyrians in their panic were ready to believe the worst; they bound the statue of Apollo with a golden chain which they attached to the altar of Hercules, the deity to whom they had consecrated their city, in the hope that he would hold Apollo back. The statue has been brought from Syracuse and erected in the land of their forefathers by the Carthaginians, who had not decorated Carthage itself more lavishly than Tyre with the many spoils taken from cities which they had captured. Some also advocated the revival of a religious rite which had been discontinued for many generations and which I certainly would not have thought to be at all acceptable to the gods – namely the sacrifice of a free-born male child to Saturn. (Such sacrilege – to use a more appropriate word than sacrifice – the Carthaginians inherited from their founders, and they are said to have continued the practice right down to the time of their city's destruction.) Had it not been vetoed by the elders, whose judgement carried weight in all matters, cruel superstition would have triumphed over civilized behaviour.

However, the urgency of the situation (more efficacious than any art) provided some novel means of defence beyond the conventional ones. To hamper the ships that approached the walls they had lashed stout beams to ropes; moving the beams forward with an engine, they would suddenly slacken the ropes and drop them on the ships. Hooks and blades hanging from the beams would also injure either the marines or the actual vessels. Furthermore, they would heat bronze shields in a blazing fire, fill them with hot sand and boiling excrement and suddenly hurl them from the walls. None of their deterrents aroused greater fear than this. The hot sand would make its way between the breastplate and the body; there was no way to shake it out and it would burn through whatever it touched. The soldiers would throw away their weapons, tear off all their

protective clothing and thus expose themselves to wounds without being able to retaliate. The 'crows' and 'iron hands' let
down from the engines also eliminated a large number of them.

At this point a weary Alexander had decided to raise the siege
and head for Egypt. After sweeping through Asia at a headlong
pace he was now detained before the walls of a single city, with
so many magnificent opportunities lost. Yet it was as disgraceful
for him to leave a failure as to linger there; he thought, too, that
his reputation would suffer – his reputation which had gained
him more conquests than military action – if he left Tyre as
witness that he could be beaten. To leave nothing untried,
he ordered more ships to be brought up and manned with
hand-picked infantrymen. Now it also happened that a sea-
creature of extraordinary size, its back protruding above the
waves, came to rest its huge body on the mole which the Macedonians had laid. Both sides caught sight of it as it parted the
water and raised itself up. Then it submerged once more at the
head of the mole, and alternately rearing most of its body above
the waves and diving beneath the surface it finally went under
not far from the city's fortifications. The sight of the creature
cheered both sides. According to the Macedonian interpretation, it had pointed out the path the mole should take. According to the Tyrians, Neptune, exacting vengeance for the
occupation of the sea, had snatched the beast away, which
meant the mole was sure to collapse shortly. Exhilarated by the
omen, they turned to feasting and excessive drinking and at
sunrise they unsteadily boarded their vessels, which they had
decorated with flowers and wreaths – so premature were they
not only in seeing an omen of their victory but in actually
celebrating it!

Now it so happened that the king had ordered the fleet to be
moved in the other direction, leaving thirty smaller vessels on
the beach. The Tyrians captured two of these and struck sheer
panic into the others until Alexander, hearing the shouts of his
men, eventually brought the fleet to the beach from which the
commotion had come. The first of the Macedonian ships to
appear was a quinquereme superior to the others in speed, and
when the Tyrian vessels sighted it two of them charged against

its sides from opposite directions. The quinquereme turned on one of these, to find itself rammed by the enemy's prow, but the Macedonian vessel in turn grappled this ship. The other Tyrian ship, which was not caught up and had a free run, began a charge at the quinquereme's other flank, at which point a trireme of Alexander's fleet, arriving very opportunely on the scene, charged into the ship, bearing down on the quinquereme with such violence that the Tyrian helmsman was hurled into the sea from the stern. More Macedonian ships then appeared and the king also came up. The Tyrians backed water, with difficulty retrieved their entangled ship, and all their vessels retreated to the harbour together. The king followed up swiftly, and though unable to enter the harbour because projectiles kept him away from the walls, he still managed to sink or capture nearly all the enemy ships.

The men were then given two days' rest, after which they were ordered to bring up the fleet and siege engines simultaneously so that Alexander could press his advantage at all points against a demoralized enemy. The king himself climbed the highest siege tower. His courage was great, but the danger greater for, conspicuous in his royal insignia and flashing armour, he was the prime target of enemy missiles. And his actions in the engagement were certainly spectacular. He transfixed with his spear many of the defenders on the walls, and some he threw headlong after striking them in hand-to-hand combat with his sword or shield, for the tower from which he fought practically abutted the enemy walls. By now the repeated battering of the rams had loosened the joints in the stones and the defensive walls had fallen; the fleet had entered the port; and some Macedonians had made their way on to the towers the enemy had abandoned.

The Tyrians were crushed by so many simultaneous reverses. Some sought refuge in the temples as suppliants while others locked their doors and anticipated the enemy by a death of their own choosing. Others again charged into the enemy, determined that their deaths should count for something. But the majority took to the rooftops, showering stones and whatever happened to be to hand on the approaching Macedonians.

Alexander ordered all but those who had fled to the temples

to be put to death and the buildings to be set on fire. Although these orders were made public by heralds, no Tyrian under arms deigned to seek protection from the gods. Young boys and girls had filled the temples, but the men all stood in the vestibules of their own homes ready to face the fury of their enemy. Many, however, found safety with the Sidonians among the Macedonian troops. Although these had entered the city with the conquerors, they remained aware that they were related to the Tyrians (they believed Agenor had founded both their cities) and so they secretly gave many of them protection and took them to their boats, on which they were hidden and transported to Sidon. Fifteen thousand were rescued from a violent death by such subterfuge. The extent of the bloodshed can be judged from the fact that 6,000 fighting men were slaughtered within the city's fortifications. It was a sad spectacle that the furious king then provided for the victors: 2,000 Tyrians, who had survived the rage of the tiring Macedonians, now hung nailed to crosses all along the huge expanse of the beach. The Carthaginian ambassadors Alexander spared, but he subjoined a formal declaration of war (a war which the pressures of the moment postponed). (Curtius)

Alexander now decided to direct his expedition towards Egypt. The rest of what is known as Syrian Palestine had already surrendered to him. However, a eunuch named Batis, who ruled over Gaza, would not submit to Alexander, and resolved that he would not allow him into the city. Batis had, some time previously, laid in ample provisions for a long siege and put together a force of Arab mercenaries, believing that his territory could not be taken by force.

Gaza is situated approximately two and a half miles from the sea, and is approached through deep sand, while the sea near the city is full of shallows. It was a large city, perched on a steep hill and surrounded by a strong wall; the last city at the edge of the desert, as one goes from Phoenicia into Egypt.

On his arrival at the city Alexander set up camp straight away where the wall seemed most open to attack and gave orders for the siege engines to be put together, only to be advised by his engineers that the steepness of the hill would make it impossible to take the city by force. Nevertheless, Alexander believed that these difficulties actually made the capture of the city even more essential as such unexpected success would strike terrible fear into his enemies, whereas failure would bring disgrace upon him when reports of it reached the Greeks and Darius. He therefore resolved to encircle the city with a mound of earth, so as to allow the siege engines to attack the wall from an equal height; his main target was the southern section of wall, which seemed the most easily assailable. When the Macedonians thought the mound was high enough, they positioned the siege engines on top of it, bringing them up against the fortifications. At the same time, Alexander was carrying out a sacrifice. Wearing the sacrificial garlands, he was just about to offer the first victim of the rites, when a bird of prey flew over the altar and dropped on to his head a stone that it had been carrying in its talons. Aristander the seer answered Alexander's enquiry about the meaning of the bird's omen with the reply, 'O King, you will capture the city, but for today you must stand guard over yourself.'

For some time Alexander listened to this advice and kept himself by the siege engines, out of range. However, a powerful attack was launched from the city and the Arabs tried to set fire to the siege engines, while also attacking the defending Macedonians beneath them from above, driving them back over the mound they had constructed. At this, Alexander went against the seer's instructions, either intentionally or because he was so shocked by events that he forgot the omen. Leading in his Guards, he came to the help of the Macedonians where the pressure was greatest and managed to prevent a shameful retreat from the mound, although he was himself wounded by a shot from a catapult which went right through his shield and breastplate into his shoulder. Nevertheless, as he realized that Aristander's prophecy about the wound had been confirmed, he rejoiced, believing that Aristander had also confirmed the capture of the city.

Alexander's wound didn't heal properly for some time. Meanwhile the siege engines with which he had captured Tyre and which had been sent for by sea arrived. He then ordered his men to build a mound two furlongs wide and 250 feet high around the city and, when the siege engines, now deployed on top of it had done serious damage to the wall, underground passages were dug at various points and the earth removed in secret, so that the unsupported wall collapsed. Firing their missiles, the Macedonians now took control of a large area, driving back those who were defending the towers, although the people of the city still managed to repel three attacks in spite of their large number of dead and wounded. However, on the fourth attempt, Alexander led in the Macedonian phalanx from all sides and pulled down the part of the wall which was already undermined, while also causing considerable damage to the section that had been bombarded by the siege engines. Ladders could now be placed on the fallen fortifications to allow easy access for the attackers. As the ladders were positioned against the wall, fierce competition broke out among those Macedonians who laid claim to bravery as to who would be first to reach the top. It was in fact, Neoptolemus, a Companion from the family of the Aeacidae, who was first to do so, and he was followed by battalion after battalion of men, together with their com-manders. As soon as some of the Macedonians were inside the fortifications, they tore down all the gates they came across, opening up the city to the entire army.

Even though their city was now taken, the people of Gaza stood together and fought, keeping to their battle positions until all of them were dead. Alexander sold the women and children as slaves, while the city became a garrison town for his campaign, having been repopulated with people from the neighbouring tribes. (Arrian)

The Egyptians had long been opposed to the power of the Persians, believing that their rule had been avaricious and arro-gant, and Alexander's prospective arrival had inspired them to hope, for they had gladly welcomed even Amyntas, coming as a deserter with power that had no firm basis. Consequently a huge crowd had gathered at Pelusium, the point at which Alexander seemed likely to enter Egypt; and in fact he arrived in that area of the country now called 'Alexander's Camp' six days after moving his troops from Gaza. He then ordered his infantry to head for Pelusium, and he himself sailed up the Nile with a select troop of light-armed soldiers. The Persians had been thoroughly shaken by the Egyptian uprising and they did not dare to await his arrival. Alexander was not far from Memphis, command of which had been left to Darius' lieutenant, Mazaces. Mazaces surrendered to him all the gold he had – more than 800 talents' worth – and all the royal furniture. From Memphis Alexander sailed upstream and penetrated into the interior of Egypt where, after settling administrative matters without tampering with Egyptian traditions, he decided to visit the oracle of Jupiter Ammon. The journey that had to be made could scarcely be managed even by a small band of soldiers lightly armed: land and sky lack moisture; the sands lie flat and barren, and when they are seared by the blazing sun the ground swelters and burns the feet and the heat is intolerable. Apart from the high temperatures and dryness of the terrain, one also had to contend with the tenacious quality of the sand, which, because of its depth and the fact that it gives way to the tread, is difficult to negotiate on foot.

The Egyptians, in fact, exaggerated these difficulties, but Alexander was nevertheless goaded by an overwhelming desire to visit the temple of Jupiter – dissatisfied with elevation on the mortal level, he either considered, or wanted others to believe, that Jupiter was his ancestor. So he sailed downstream to Lake Mareotis with the men he had decided to take with him, and there ambassadors from Cyrene brought him gifts, asking for peace and requesting that he visit their cities. Alexander accepted the gifts, concluded treaties with them, and resumed his proposed journey. The first and second day the difficulties seemed bearable, for they had yet to reach the vast stretches of naked desert, though even now the earth was barren and lifeless. However, when plains covered with deep sand appeared, it was as if they were entering a vast sea and their eyes vainly looked for land – no tree was to be seen, not a trace of cultivated soil. They had also run out of water, which had been carried in skins by camels, and in the arid soil and burning sand not a drop was to be found. The sun had also parched everything, and their throats were dry and burned, when suddenly – whether it was a gift of the gods or pure chance – clouds shrouded the sky and hid the sun, providing enormous relief for them, exhausted as they were by the heat, even despite the absence of water. In fact, though, high winds now showered down generous quantities of rain, of which each man collected his own supply, some of them, wild with thirst, attempting to catch it with gaping mouths.

After four days in the desert wastes, they found themselves not far from the site of the oracle. Here a number of crows met the column, flying ahead of the front standards at a slow pace, occasionally settling on the ground, when the column's advance was relatively slow, and then again taking off as if they were going ahead to show the way. At last the Macedonians reached the area consecrated to the god, which, incredibly, located though it is among the desert wastes, is so well screened on all sides by encircling tree branches that the rays of the sun barely penetrate the shade, and its woods are sustained by a wealth of fresh-water springs. The climate, too, is amazingly temperate, with the mildness of springtime, providing a healthy atmosphere through all the seasons of the year. Next to the shrine to the east are the nearest Ethiopian tribes; to the south they face Arab peoples called Trogodytes, whose territory extends right to the Red Sea; to the west live other Ethiopians called Simui; and to the north are the Nasamones, a tribe of the Syrtes who make a living by looting ships (they haunt the shore line and their knowledge of the shallows enables them to seize vessels stranded by the tide).

The people who inhabit the wooded area are called Hammonii; they live in scattered huts, and regard the centre of the wood, which is encircled by three walls, as a citadel. The first rampart surrounded the old palace of their kings; behind the second lived their wives, children and concubines, and the oracle of the god is also in this area; the outermost fortifications were the homes of the palace attendants and bodyguards. There is also a second wood of Ammon with a fountain called 'The Water of the Sun' at its centre. At sunrise it runs lukewarm, and yet at midday, despite the inordinate heat, it is cold, warming up towards evening and growing boiling hot at midnight. Then, as dawn approaches, it loses much of its nocturnal heat until at daybreak it drops back to its original lukewarm temperature. The image worshipped as divine does not have the appearance commonly accorded deities by artists; it most resembles a navel and is composed of an emerald and other jewels. When an oracular response is sought, priests carry this along in a gilded boat from which a large number of silver cups hang on both sides, and married and unmarried women follow, singing in traditional fashion some artless song by which they believe an infallible answer is elicited from Jupiter.

On this occasion, as the king approached, he was addressed as 'son' by the oldest of the priests, who claimed that this title was bestowed on him by his father Jupiter. Forgetting his mortal state, Alexander said he accepted and acknowledged the title, and he proceeded to ask whether he was fated to rule over the entire world. The priest, who was as ready as anyone else to flatter him, answered that he was going to rule over all the earth. After this Alexander went on to inquire whether his father's murderers had all received their punishment. The priest's answer was that no harm could come to his father from anybody's wrongdoing, but that as far as Philip was concerned all had paid the penalty; and he added that he would remain undefeated until he went to join the gods. Alexander thereupon offered sacrifice, presented gifts both to the priests and to the god, and also allowed his friends to consult Jupiter on their own account. Their only question was whether the god authorized their according divine honours to their king, and this, too, so the priest replied, would be agreeable to Jupiter.

Someone making a sound and honest judgement of the oracle's reliability might well have found these responses disingenuous, but fortune generally makes those whom she has compelled to put their trust in her alone more thirsty for glory than capable of coping with it. So Alexander did not just permit but actually ordered the title 'Jupiter's son' to be accorded to himself, and while he wanted such a title to add lustre to his achievements he really detracted from them. Furthermore, although it is true that the Macedonians were accustomed to monarchy, they lived in the shadow of liberty more than other races, and so they rejected his pretensions to immortality with greater obstinacy than was good either for themselves or their king.

Returning from the shrine of Ammon, Alexander came to Lake Mareotis, not far from the island of Pharos. After an examination of the area's natural features he had at first decided to locate a new city on the island itself, but it then became apparent that it had not the capacity for a large settlement, and so he chose for his city the present site of Alexandria (which draws its name from its founder). Taking in all the land between the lake and the sea he marked out an eighty-stade circuit for the walls, and left men to supervise construction of the city. He then set out for Memphis, for the desire had come over him (understandable, indeed, but ill-timed) to visit not just the Egyptian interior but Ethiopia as well. In his longing to explore antiquities, the famous palace of Memnon and Tithonus was drawing him almost beyond the boundaries of the sun. (Curtius)

5. THE PERSIAN CAMPAIGN (3)
– VICTORY IN PERSIA

Alexander departs from Egypt and waits at Tyre for news of Darius. Leaving Tyre, he crosses the Euphrates and the Tigris, and prepares for battle at Gaugamela. In a massive victory Alexander gains control of the Persian empire, although Darius himself once again manages to escape. Alexander then marches south and is given a majestic welcome in Babylon, where he rests for five weeks and rebuilds the temples. At Susa he sits in Darius' throne. Finally he takes control of Persepolis, the centre of the Persian empire, without resistance. His troops loot the city and Alexander burns down the palace, the reasons for which remain uncertain. In pursuit of Darius, Alexander moves eastwards, only to find him already dead, stabbed to death by his own courtiers. He gives Darius a royal burial at Persia and, donning part of the royal costume, settles affairs in his new Persian kingdom.

Meanwhile Alexander, after subduing the whole region which lay on his line of march between the Tigris and the Euphrates, resumed his advance against Darius, who was on his way to meet him with a million men.* On this march one of his companions mentioned to Alexander to amuse him that the camp followers had divided themselves for sport into two armies, and had appointed a general and commander for each, one of whom they had named Alexander and the other Darius. At first they had only pelted one another with clods of earth, then they had

---

* A propagandist figure. Modern estimates put the Persian strength at a maximum of 100,000 infantry and 34,000 cavalry.

come to blows with their fists, and finally, inflamed with the heat of battle, they had fought in earnest with stones and clubs. More and more men had joined in, until at last it had become hard to separate them. When Alexander heard of this, he ordered the leaders to be matched so as to fight in single combat: he himself gave weapons and armour to his namesake, and Philotas gave them to the so-called Darius. The whole army watched this contest and saw in it something of an omen for their own campaign. After a strenuous fight, 'Alexander' finally prevailed, and received as a prize twelve villages and the right to wear the Persian dress. This at least is the story we have from Eratosthenes.

The great battle that was fought against Darius did not take place at Arbela, as the majority of writers say, but at Gaugamela. The word signifies 'the house of the camel': one of the ancient kings of this country escaped the pursuit of his enemies on a swift camel and gave the animal a home there, setting aside various revenues and the produce of several villages to maintain it. It happened that in the month of Boedromion, about the same time as the beginning of the festival of the mysteries at Athens, there was an eclipse of the moon. On the eleventh night after this, by which time the two armies were in sight of one another, Darius kept his troops under arms and held a review of them by torchlight. Alexander allowed his Macedonians to sleep, but himself spent the night in front of his tent in the company of his diviner Aristander, with whom he performed certain mysterious and sacred ceremonies and offered sacrifice to the god Fear. Meanwhile some of the older of his companions, and Parmenion in particular, looked out over the plain between the river Niphates and the Gordyaean mountains and saw the entire plain agleam with the watch-fires of the barbarians, while from their camp there arose the confused and indistinguishable murmur of myriads of voices, like the distant roar of a vast ocean. They were filled with amazement at the sight and remarked to one another that it would be an overwhelmingly difficult task to defeat an enemy of such strength by engaging him by day. They therefore went to the king as soon as he had performed his sacrifice and tried to persuade him to attack by night, so as to conceal from his men the most terrifying element in the coming struggle, that is, the odds against them. It was then that Alexander gave them his celebrated answer, 'I will not steal my victory.' Some of his companions thought this an immature and empty boast on the part of a young man who was merely joking in the presence of danger. But others interpreted it as meaning that he had confidence in his present situation and that he had correctly judged the future. In other words, he was determined that if Darius were defeated, he should have no cause to summon up courage for another attempt: he was not to be allowed to blame darkness and night for his failure on this occasion, as at Issus he had blamed the narrow mountain passes and the sea. Certainly Darius would never abandon the war for lack of arms or of troops, when he could draw upon such a vast territory and such immense reserves of manpower. He would only do so when he had lost courage and become convinced of his inferiority in consequence of an unmistakable defeat suffered in broad daylight.

When his friends had gone, Alexander lay down in his tent and is said to have passed the rest of the night in a deeper sleep than usual. At any rate when his officers came to him in the early morning, they were astonished to find him not yet awake, and on their own responsibility gave out orders for the soldiers to take breakfast before anything else was done. Then, as time was pressing, Parmenion entered Alexander's tent, stood by his couch and called him two or three times by name: when he had roused him, he asked how he could possibly sleep as if he were already victorious, instead of being about to fight the greatest battle of his life. Alexander smiled and said, 'Why not? Do you not see that we have already won the battle, now that we are delivered from roving around these endless devastated plains, and chasing this Darius, who will never stand and fight?' And indeed not only beforehand, but at the very height of the battle Alexander displayed the supremacy and steadfastness of a man who is confident of the soundness of his judgement.

As the action developed, the left wing under Parmenion was driven back and found itself hard pressed, first by a violent charge from the Bactrian cavalry, and later by an outflanking movement when Mazaeus sent a detachment of horsemen to ride round the line and attack the troops who were guarding the Macedonian baggage. Parmenion, who was disconcerted by both these manoeuvres, sent messengers to warn Alexander that his camp and his baggage train were lost, unless he could immediately move strong reinforcements from the front to protect his rear. It so happened that at that moment Alexander was about to give the signal to the right wing, which he commanded, to attack: when he received this message, he exclaimed that Parmenion must have lost his wits and forgotten in his agitation that the victors will always take possession of their enemy's baggage in any event, and that the losers must not concern themselves with their property or their slaves, but only with how to fight bravely and die with honour.

After he had sent this message to Parmenion, he put on his helmet. He was already wearing the rest of his armour when he left his tent, a tunic made in Sicily which was belted around his waist and over this a thickly quilted linen corselet, which had been among the spoils captured at Issus. His helmet, the work of Theophilus, was made of steel which gleamed like polished silver, and to this was fitted a steel gorget set with precious stones. His sword, which was a gift from the king of Citium, was a marvel of lightness and tempering, and he had trained himself to use this as his principal weapon in hand-to-hand fighting. He also wore a cloak which was more ornate than the rest of his armour. It had been made by Helicon, an artist of earlier times, and presented to Alexander as a mark of honour by the city of Rhodes, and this too he was in the habit of wearing in battle. While he was drawing up the phalanx in formation, reviewing the troops, or giving out orders, he rode another horse to spare Bucephalus, who was by now past his prime: but when he was about to go into action Bucephalus would be led up, and he would mount him and at once begin the attack. (Plutarch)

In the meantime Alexander's cavalry commander, Menidas, had arrived with a few squadrons to bring help to the baggage (whether this was his own idea or done on Alexander's orders is unknown), but he was unable to hold out against an attack from the Cadusians and Scythians. With no real attempt at fighting he retreated to the king, less a champion of the baggage than a witness to its loss! Indignation had already crushed Alexander's resolve, and he was afraid – not without justification – that concern with recovering the baggage might draw his men from the fight. Accordingly he sent Aretes, the leader of the lancers called the *Sarisophoroi*, against the Scythians.

Meanwhile, after causing havoc in Alexander's front lines, the chariots had now charged the phalanx, and the Macedonians received the charge with a firm resolve, permitting them to penetrate to the middle of the column. Their formation resembled a rampart; after creating an unbroken line of spears, they stabbed the flanks of the horses from both sides as they charged recklessly ahead. Then they began to surround the chariots and to throw the fighters out of them. Horses and charioteers fell in huge numbers, covering the battlefield. The charioteers could not control the terrified animals, which, frequently tossing their necks, had not only thrown off their yokes but also overturned the chariots, and wounded horses were trying to drag along dead ones, unable to stay in one place in their panic and yet too weak to go forward. Even so a few chariots escaped to the back line, inflicting a pitiful death on those they encountered. The ground was littered with the several limbs of soldiers and, as there was no pain while the wounds were still warm, the men did not in fact drop their weapons, despite the mutilation and their weakness, until they dropped dead from loss of blood.

In the meantime Aretes had killed the leader of the Scythians who were looting the baggage. When they panicked he put greater pressure on them, until on Darius' orders some Bactrians appeared to change the fortunes of the battle. Many Macedonians were crushed in the first onslaught, and more fled back to Alexander. Then, raising a shout as victors do, the Persians made a ferocious rush at their enemy in the belief that they had been crushed in every corner. Alexander reproached and encouraged his terrified men, single-handedly reviving the flagging battle and then, their confidence finally restored, he ordered them to charge the enemy.

The Persian line was thinner on the right wing, since it was from there that the Bactrians had withdrawn to attack the baggage; Alexander advanced on these weakened ranks, causing great loss of Persian life with his attack. The Persians on the left wing, however, positioned themselves to his rear as he fought, hoping that he could be boxed in. He would have faced terrible danger, pinned in the middle as he was, had not the Agrianian cavalry come galloping to assault the Persians surrounding the king and forced them to turn towards them by cutting into their rear. There was confusion on both sides. Alexander had Persians before and behind him, and those putting pressure on his rear were themselves under attack from the Agrianian cavalry; the Bactrians on their return from looting the enemy baggage could not form up again; and at the same time several detachments broken off from the main body were fighting wherever chance had brought them into contact.

With the main bodies almost together, the two kings spurred on their men to battle. There were more Persian dead now, and the number of wounded on each side was about equal. Darius was riding in his chariot, Alexander on horseback, and both had a guard of hand-picked men who had no regard for their own lives – with their king lost they had neither the desire nor the opportunity to reach safety, and each man thought it a noble fate to meet his end before the eyes of his king. But the men facing the greatest danger were, in fact, those given the best protection, since each soldier sought for himself the glory of killing the enemy king.

Now whether their eyes were deceiving them or they really did sight it, Alexander's Guards believed they saw an eagle gently hovering just above the king's head, frightened neither by the clash of arms nor the groans of the dying, and for a long time it was observed around Alexander's horse, apparently hanging in the air rather than flying. At all events the prophet Aristander, dressed in white and with a laurel branch in his right hand, kept pointing out to the soldiers, who were preoccupied with the fight, the bird which he claimed was an infallible omen of victory. The men who had been terrified moments before were now fired with tremendous enthusiasm and confidence for the fight, especially after Darius' charioteer, who drove the horses, seated before the king, was run through by a spear. Persians and Macedonians alike were convinced that it was the king who had been killed, and though the fortunes of the battle were, in fact, still even, Darius' 'kinsmen' and squires caused consternation almost throughout the battlefield with their mournful wailing and wild shouts and groans. The left wing was routed and abandoned the king's chariot which the close-formed ranks on the right received into the middle of their column.

It is said that Darius drew his scimitar and considered avoiding ignominious flight by an honourable death, but highly visible as he was in his chariot, he felt ashamed to abandon his forces when they were not all committed to leaving the battle. While he wavered between hope and despair, the Persians gradually began to give ground and broke ranks.

Alexander changed horses – he had exhausted several – and began to stab at the faces of the Persians still resisting and at the backs of those who ran. It was no longer a battle but a massacre, and Darius also turned his chariot in flight. The victor kept hard on the heels of his fleeing enemy, but a dust cloud rising into the air obstructed visibility; the Macedonians wandered around like people in the dark, converging only when they recognized a voice or heard a signal. But they could hear the sound of reins time and time again lashing the chariot horses, the only trace they had of the fleeing king.

On the left wing, which (as stated above) was under Parmenion's command, the fortunes of the battle were very different for both sides. Mazaeus exerted pressure on the Macedonian cavalry squadrons by making a violent attack on them with all his horse and, having superior numbers, he had already begun to encircle their infantry when Parmenion ordered some horsemen to report their critical position to Alexander and tell him that flight was inevitable unless help came quickly. The king had already covered a great distance in his pursuit of the fleeing Persians when the bad news from Parmenion arrived. His mounted men were told to pull up their horses and the infantry column came to a halt. Alexander was furious that victory was being snatched out of his hands and that Darius was more successful in flight than he himself was in pursuit.

Meanwhile news of his king's defeat had reached Mazaeus, and he, in his alarm at his side's reverse of fortune, began to relax his pressure on the dispirited Macedonians despite his superior strength. Although ignorant of why the attack had lost its impetus, Parmenion quickly seized the chance of victory. He had the Thessalian cavalry summoned to him and said, 'Do you see how after making a furious attack on us a moment ago those men are retreating in sudden panic? It must be that our king's good fortune has brought victory for us too. The battlefield is completely covered with Persian dead. What are you waiting for? Aren't you a match even for soldiers in flight?'

His words rang true, and fresh hope revived their drooping spirits. At a gallop they charged their enemy, who started to give ground not just gradually but swiftly, and all that prevented this being termed a flight was the fact that the Persians had not yet turned their backs. However, since he was ignorant of how the king was faring on the right wing, Parmenion checked his men and, given the opportunity to retreat, Mazaeus crossed the Tigris – not taking a direct route but a longer, circuitous one which accordingly offered greater safety – and entered Babylon with the remnants of the defeated army. (Curtius)

Darius headed straight from the battle towards Media, passing through the mountains of Armenia as he fled. The Bactrian cavalry, who had fought alongside him, and some of the Persians – his royal kinsmen and a few of the Royal Guards – went with him. Also with him were about 2,000 of the foreign mercenaries led by Paron of Phocis and Glaucus of Aetolia. He directed his retreat towards Medea in the belief that after the battle Alexander would advance towards Susa and Babylon. The road that led there passed through a populated region and was wide and suitable for transporting the baggage, whereas the one leading to Media would be difficult for a large army. Moreover, Babylon and Susa seemed to be the likely prizes the victorious Macedonians would want to claim.

Darius was correct and Alexander headed straight for Babylon on leaving Arbela. As he drew close to Babylon, his forces prepared for battle, he was met by its people together with their priests and magistrates, each of them bearing gifts, who handed their city over to him, along with its citadel and treasures. He then entered Babylon and instructed the Babylonians to rebuild the temples destroyed by Xerxes, especially the temple of Bel, the god whom they most revered. Mazaeus was appointed as satrap of Babylon, Apollodorus of Amphipolis as general of the soldiers to be left behind with Mazaeus, and Asclepiodorus, son of Philo, as collector of the tribute. Mithrines, who had surrendered the acropolis of Sardis to Alexander, was sent to be satrap of Armenia. It was also here in Babylon that Alexander came upon the Chaldaeans, and he was to heed their counsel in religious matters, especially when it came to the sacrifices to Bel that they prescribed.

Alexander then set out for Susa, and was met on the way by its satrap's son and a letter-bearer sent by Philoxenus, whom he had dispatched to Susa immediately after the battle. In his letter Philoxenus had written that the people of Susa had handed over the city to Alexander, and that all their riches had been secured for him. It took Alexander twenty days to reach Susa from Babylon and, on his arrival in the city, he was presented with a treasure amounting to around 50,000 silver talents, as well as other royal valuables. Along with these he also took possession of the many treasures that Xerxes had brought back with him from Greece; in particular, the bronze statues of Harmodius and Aristogeiton, which now stand in Athens in the Cerameicus. This is situated on the way up to the Acropolis, just opposite the Metröon and not far from the altar of the Eudanemi – an altar which, as is known by any initiate of the Mysteries of the Eleusinian Twin Goddesses,* is on flat ground. (Arrian)

When Alexander advanced beyond Susa, he found the province of Persis difficult to penetrate: not only was the country mountainous, but it was defended by the bravest of the Persians since Darius had taken refuge there. In spite of these obstacles

---

* Demeter and Persephone.

Alexander found a guide who showed him the way by making a short diversion. This man had a Lycian father and a Persian mother and spoke both Greek and Persian, and it was to him, so the story goes, that the Pythian priestess had referred when she prophesied while Alexander was still a boy that a *lykos* (wolf) would guide him on his march against the Persians. During the advance across Persis the Greeks massacred great numbers of their prisoners, and Alexander has himself recorded that he gave orders for the Persians to be slaughtered because he thought that such an example would help his cause. It is said that in Persepolis, the capital of the province, he found as much gold as he had in Susa, and that it required 2,000 pairs of mules and 500 camels to carry away the furniture and other treasures that were found there.

It was in Persepolis that Alexander saw a gigantic statue of Xerxes. This had been toppled from its pedestal and heedlessly left on the ground by a crowd of soldiers, as they forced their way into the palace, and Alexander stopped and spoke to it as though it were alive. 'Shall I pass by and leave you lying there because of the expedition you led against Greece, or shall I set you up again because of your magnanimity and your virtues in other respects?' For a long while he gazed at the statue and reflected in silence, and then went on his way. It was by then winter, and he stayed in Persepolis for four months to allow his soldiers time to rest. It is said that when he first took his seat on the royal throne under the golden canopy, Demaratus the Corinthian, who was much attached to Alexander, as he had been to his father, began to weep, as old men are apt to do, and exclaimed that any Greek who had died before that day had missed one of the greatest pleasures in life by not seeing Alexander seated on the throne of Darius.

In the spring Alexander again took the field against Darius, but a short while before it so happened that he accepted an invitation to a drinking party held by some of his companions, and on this occasion a number of women came to meet their lovers and joined in the drinking. The most celebrated of these was Thais, an Athenian, at that time the mistress of the Ptolemy who later became the ruler of Egypt. As the drinking went on,

Thais delivered a speech which was intended partly as a graceful compliment to Alexander and partly to amuse him. What she said was typical of the spirit of Athens, but hardly in keeping with her own situation. She declared that all the hardships she had endured in wandering about Asia had been amply repaid on that day, when she found herself revelling luxuriously in the splendid palace of the Persians, but that it would be an even sweeter pleasure to end the party by going out and setting fire to the palace of Xerxes, who had laid Athens in ashes. She wanted to put a torch to the building herself in full view of Alexander, so that posterity should know that the women who followed Alexander had taken a more terrible revenge for the wrongs of Greece than all the famous commanders of earlier times by land or sea. Her speech was greeted with wild applause and the king's companions excitedly urged him on until at last he allowed himself to be persuaded, leaped to his feet, and with a garland on his head and a torch in his hand led the way. The other revellers followed, shouting and dancing, and surrounded the palace, and those of the Macedonians who had heard what was afoot delightedly ran up bringing torches with them. They did this because they hoped that the act of burning and destroying the palace signified that Alexander's thoughts were turned towards home, and that he was not planning to settle among the barbarians. According to a number of historians it was in this way that the palace was burned down, that is on impulse, but there are others who maintain that it was an act of deliberate policy. However this may be, it is agreed that Alexander quickly repented and gave orders for the fire to be put out. (Plutarch)

Alexander goes into Media, in pursuit of Darius, and rests at Rhagae, where he waits for news.

At this point Bagistanes, a Babylonian nobleman, arrived from Darius' camp to see Alexander, together with Antibelus, one of Mazaeus' sons. They informed Alexander that the following people had arrested Darius: Nabarzanes, the commander of the cavalry that had fled with Darius; Bessus, satrap of Bactria; and

Barsaentes, satrap of Arachotia and Drangiana. On hearing this news Alexander forged ahead even faster: without even awaiting the return of Coenus' men from their foraging, he took only the Companions, the mounted scouts and a select group comprising the strongest and lightest of the infantry. Craterus was put in command of those left behind, with instructions to follow at a moderate pace, while those who accompanied Alexander carried only their weapons and enough food for two days. Having marched for a whole night and morning, he rested his troops for a short while at midday, before pressing on through another night to reach Bagistanes' camp at daybreak. The enemy had fled. Alexander learnt that Darius had been arrested and taken away in a covered wagon, while Bessus, who had seized control in his place, was being hailed as commander by the Bactrian cavalry and by all of the Persians who had escaped with Darius, except for Artabazus and his sons, and the Greek mercenaries, who had remained loyal to Darius. Since they were unable to prevent what had happened, they had left the main road and headed into the hills by themselves, unwilling to take part in what Bessus' supporters were doing. The men who had seized Darius had decided that they would hand Darius over in order to obtain some benefit for themselves if they discovered that Alexander was in pursuit; whereas, if they were informed that he had turned back, they would gather up as large an army as they could and fight together to save their empire. For now Bessus was in command, both because of his relationship to Darius and because the coup had taken place within his satrapy.

This information sharpened Alexander's resolve to press on with his pursuit. Although his men and horses were already exhausted by their relentless effort, he led them on, covering a huge distance during the night and the following day until, at midday, he arrived at a village where Darius' captors had made camp the day before. On learning that the Persians had decided to continue their journey by night, he asked the locals whether they knew of a shortcut to reach those who were fleeing from him. They replied that they did know a way, but that it was deserted due to lack of water. In spite of this, Alexander ordered them to lead him along this route and, realizing that the foot soldiers would not be able to follow with any speed, he had around 500 of the cavalry dismount. He then chose the most resilient officers from among the infantry and other groups and ordered them to mount the horses, still carrying their usual weapons. Meanwhile he ordered Nicanor, the commander of the Guards, and Attalus, the commander of the Agrianes, to lead the remainder of the men along the road by which Bessus' men had travelled with their men equipped as lightly as possible, while the rest of the infantry were to follow in their usual formation. Alexander himself led his men out at dusk with such speed that they covered around fifty miles during the night and came upon the Persians at the very break of day. They were marching in no particular order and without their arms, so that only a few of them mustered up some resistance, while the majority fled the moment that they saw Alexander, before he had even got close. Even those who had turned to defend themselves ran away once there were a few casualties. At first Bessus and his companions tried to take Darius along with them in the covered wagon; but, as Alexander approached, Nazarbanes and Barsaentes wounded Darius and left him behind, fleeing with 600 cavalry. Shortly afterwards, before Alexander was able to see him, Darius died from his wounds.

Alexander then sent Darius' body to Persepolis with orders that it should be buried in the royal tombs, just like the kings who had preceded him. (Arrian)

Meanwhile he himself with the flower of his army pressed on into Hyrcania. Here he came in sight of a bay of the open sea which appeared to be as large as the Black Sea, and was sweeter than the Mediterranean. He could not obtain any certain information about it, but guessed that it was probably a stagnant overflow from Lake Maeotis. However, various geographers had already discovered the truth and many years before Alexander's expedition they had recorded their conclusion that this was the most northerly of four gulfs which run inland from the outer Ocean and was called the Hyrcanian or Caspian Sea. In this neighbourhood the barbarians surprised the grooms who were leading Alexander's horse Bucephalus, and captured him. Alexander was enraged and sent a herald with the threat that, unless they gave back his horse, he would exterminate the whole tribe, together with their women and children. However, when they returned with the horse and surrendered their cries to him, he treated them all kindly, and even gave a reward to the men who had captured Bucephalus.

From this point he advanced into Parthia, and it was here during a pause in the campaign that he first began to wear barbarian dress. He may have done this from a desire to adapt himself to local habits, because he understood that the sharing of race and of customs is a great step towards softening men's hearts. Alternatively, this may have been an experiment which was aimed at introducing the obeisance among the Macedonians, the first stage being to accustom them to accepting changes in his own dress and way of life. However, he did not go so far as to adopt the Median costume, which was altogether barbaric and outlandish, and he wore neither trousers, nor a sleeved vest, nor a tiara. Instead he adopted a style which was a compromise between Persian and Median costume, more modest than the first, and more stately than the second. At first he wore this only when he was in the company of barbarians or with his intimate friends indoors, but later he put it on when he was riding or giving audience in public. The sight greatly displeased the Macedonians, but they admired his other virtues so much that they considered they ought to make concessions to him in some matters which either gave him pleasure or increased his prestige. For besides all his other hardships, he had recently been wounded below the knee by an arrow which splintered the shinbone so that the fragments had to be taken out, and on another occasion he had received such a violent blow on the neck from a stone that his vision became clouded and remained so for a long time afterwards. In spite of this, he continued to expose himself unsparingly to danger: for example, he crossed the river Orexartes, which he believed to be the Tanais, routed the Scythians and pursued them for twelve miles or more, even though all this while he was suffering from an attack of dysentery. (Plutarch)

6. TO THE NORTH-EAST FRONTIERS OF THE PERSIAN EMPIRE

Heading east into modern Afghanistan, Alexander is challenged by the Persians Satibarzanes and Bessus. Meanwhile at Farah Alexander discovers a plot against his life, in which Parmenion's son Philotas is implicated. Having condemned Philotas, Alexander arranges for Parmenion, in charge of the forces at Ectabana (Hamadan), to be killed. Although it seems plausible that Philotas was indeed part of a plot, his guilt, and certainly the involvement of Parmenion, remains uncertain. Rushing on to surprise Bessus, Alexander begins his crossing of the Hindu Kush in winter. Bessus flees, his cavalry desert, and Alexander is able to travel on to Balkh unhindered. From here he heads north in pursuit of Bessus, who is handed over by his own companions. Alexander presses on and reaches the north-east frontier of the Persian empire in July 330. However, dogged by rebellions to his south, he returns to a winter camp at Bactra (also known as Zariaspa, the modern Balkh), where he is helped by the arrival of over 20,000 reinforcements from the west. At Maracanda (Samarkand), Alexander kills his friend Cleitus in a drunken quarrel and is full of remorse. The success of his campaign now increases. After various victories, the allies of Alexander's opponent Spitamenes surrender and kill their leader, while Alexander then goes on to conquer the rock fortresses of Sogdia and Sisimithres. It is here that he marries Roxane, a Persian princess famed for her beauty. It is around this time also that Callisthenes, a cousin of the philosopher Aristotle, offends Alexander by refusing to do obeisance, or proskynesis (prostrating oneself before the ruler). Alexander was trying to introduce this Persian custom for Greeks and Persians alike, even though his Greek followers would have found it demeaning. Shortly afterwards Callisthenes dies. Given the conflicting accounts concerning both the nature of his dispute with Alexander and whether he was executed or died naturally, it is not possible to reach a firm conclusion.

As Alexander was on his way to Bactra, he was informed that Satibarzanes, satrap of Aria, had slaughtered Anaxippus along with his forty men, and was arming the Arians and bringing them together at the city of Artacoana, the site of the Arian palace. As soon as he had learnt that Alexander had advanced, he had decided to go to Bessus with his forces, so that they could take whatever chance arose to attack the Macedonians together. On hearing this news, Alexander no longer followed his course to Bactra, but, leaving the rest of his army behind under the command of Craterus, took with him the Companion Cavalry, the mounted javelin men, the archers, the Agrianes and the battalions of Amyntas and Coenus, and rapidly led them against Satibarzanes and the Arians, arriving in Artacoana two days later after a journey of around seventy-five miles.

Thrown into a panic by the speed of Alexander's approach Satibarzanes fled as soon as he realized Alexander was at hand with just a few of the Arian cavalry; the bulk of his army had deserted him in his retreat, the moment they had learnt that Alexander was drawing near. Alexander's pursuit was swift and he dealt with the fugitives as he came across them: anyone revealed to have collaborated in the uprising and to have deserted their village during that period was either killed or sold into slavery. Arsaces, a Persian, was appointed as satrap of Asia, while Alexander himself now proceeded towards the country of Zarangia with all of his men, and having been rejoined by those left behind with Craterus, arrived at the palace of the Zarangians. Meanwhile Barsaentes, one of those who had joined in with the attack on the fleeing Darius, now in control of the region, fled to the Indians on the west side of the Indus on hearing of Alexander's approach. However, the Indians arrested him and sent him to Alexander, who put him to death for having been a traitor to Darius.

It was also here that Alexander learnt that Philotas, the son of Parmenion, was plotting against him. Ptolemy and Aristobulus both claim that he had already received this information in Egypt, but did not believe it for a number of reasons: their long-standing friendship; the honours which he had bestowed on Philotas' father Parmenion; and his faith in Philotas himself. Ptolemy, son of Lagus, reports that Philotas was brought before the Macedonians and defended himself against Alexander's severe accusations. Those who had reported the plot then offered a range of firm evidence against Philotas and his companions. Most damaging was their claim that Philotas had himself learnt that a plot was being hatched against Alexander, but could be proved to have kept this information from Alexander, even though he frequented his tent twice a day. The Macedonians put Philotas and all those who had taken part in this conspiracy to death with spears, while Polydamas, one of the Companions, was sent to Parmenion. He bore a letter from Alexander to the generals of Parmenion's force in Media, Cleander, Sitalces and Menidas, who executed Parmenion on his order. This may have been because it seemed impossible to Alexander that Parmenion had taken no part in the conspiracy of Philotas, his own son. Alternatively, even if he had had no part in the plot, for him to survive his son's execution would not be dangerous, for he was held in great esteem not only by Alexander, but by his army, and even by the mercenaries, whom he had often led, either in their normal duties or on the special instructions and requests of Alexander.

It is said that, at the same time, Amyntas, son of Andromenes, together with his brothers Polemon, Attalus and Simmias, were also brought before the court on charges of conspiring against Alexander, on account of their loyal friendship with Philotas. Most people found this plot all the more likely since Polemon had sought refuge with the enemy when Philotas was arrested. Nevertheless, Amyntas and his other brothers stayed behind to stand trial and the powerful defence that he gave before the Macedonians gained their acquittal. As soon as he was acquitted, he requested and was in turn granted the court's permission to go to his brother Polemon and bring him back to Alexander.

Amyntas set off the very same day and brought back Polemon, so that his own innocence now seemed to have been proven even more conclusively than before. Yet his death shortly afterwards, from an arrow wound received while he was besieging some village, meant that the only consequence of his acquittal was to die with his reputation intact.

Alexander now put two men, Hephaestion, son of Amyntor, and Cleitus, son of Dropides, in charge of the Companions, dividing the Companions in two between them; for he was unwilling for any single man, even one of his friends, to be in command of so large a cavalry, in fact, his most powerful mounted force, whose reputation was matched by its valour. With the Companions thus reorganized, he arrived among the people who used to be known as Ariaspians, but were later called the Benefactors, since they had helped Cyrus, son of Cambyses, in his attack on Scythia. Alexander had respect for these people, both because their predecessors had provided assistance to Cyrus, and because they did not share other tribes' barbaric ways of government, but had a justice system equivalent to that of the greatest of the Greeks. For these reasons, he granted them their freedom, together with as much of the neighbouring territory as they wished; even so, they asked for very little. (Arrian)

These adjustments made, Alexander appointed a satrap over the Arians and then had orders issued for a march into the land of the Arimaspi. (Even at that time they were still called the Euergetae, a name change dating from the time when they had given assistance to Cyrus' army in the form of shelter and supplies when it was ravaged by cold and shortages of food.) Four days after entering that region Alexander learned that Satibarzanes, who had defected to Bessus, had made a second incursion against the Arii with a force of cavalry. He therefore dispatched Caranus and Erigyius together with Artabazus and Andronicus, and along with them went 6,000 Greek infantry and 600 horse.

As for Alexander himself, within sixty days he drew up ordinances relating to the Euergetae, including a large financial reward for their outstanding loyalty to Cyrus. He then left the former secretary of Darius, Amedines, to govern them and proceeded to subdue the Arachosii, whose territory extends to the Pontic Sea. There he was met by the army which had been under Parmenion's command: 6,000 Macedonians, 200 noblemen and 5,000 Greeks (with 600 cavalry), undoubtedly the pick of all the king's forces. Menon was appointed governor of the Arachosii and was left a garrison of 4,000 infantry and 600 cavalry.

Alexander advanced with his army into the territory of a tribe scarcely known even to its neighbours since it had no trading connections. They are called the Parapamisadae and are a backward tribe, extremely uncivilized even for barbarians, the harshness of the environment having hardened the character of the people. Most of their territory faces the cold northern pole, but it touches Bactria to the west and extends as far as the Indian Ocean in the south. Their huts they build of brick from the foundations up and, because the country is devoid of timber (even the mountain range is bare), they employ the same brickwork right to the top of their buildings. Their structure is fairly broad at the base but gradually narrows as the work rises until it finally converges to form what looks most like a ship's keel. At this point an aperture is left to admit light from above. Such vines and trees as have been able to survive in the frozen soil the inhabitants set deep in the ground. They remain hidden beneath the surface in winter and return to the air and sunlight only when winter ends and exposes the earth. In fact, the snow cover is so thick on the ground and so hardened with ice and almost permanent frost that no trace is to be found even of birds or any other animal of the wild. The overcast daylight, which would be more accurately called a shadow of the sky, resembles night and hangs so close to the earth that nearby objects are barely visible. Cut off in this area, which was so devoid of any trace of human presence, the army faced every hardship it is possible to bear: lack of provisions, cold, fatigue, despair. The numbing cold of the snow, of which they had no experience, claimed many lives; for many others it brought frostbite to the feet and for a very large number snow blindness. It was especially deadly for men suffering from exhaustion. They stretched their fatigued bodies on the surface of the ice and, once they stopped moving, the intensity of the cold made them so stiff that all their efforts to get up again were to no avail. Their comrades would try to shake the languor from them, and the only remedy was to make them go on – only then, with the vital heat set in motion, would some energy return to their limbs.

Anyone who managed to reach the huts of the barbarians quickly recovered, but the gloom was so dense that the location of these buildings was only revealed by the smoke from them. The inhabitants had never before seen a foreigner in their lands, and the sudden sight of armed intruders almost frightened them to death. They began to bring out whatever they had in their huts, begging the Macedonians to spare their lives. The king made the round of his troops on foot, raising up some who were on the ground and using his body to lend support to others when they had difficulty keeping up. At one moment he was at the front, at another at the centre or rear of the column, multiplying for himself the hardships of the march. Finally they reached a more cultivated area where the troops were revived by a plentiful supply of provisions, while the men who had been unable to keep up also came into the camp they established there.

The force advanced from here to the Caucasus mountains, a range forming a continuous claim that splits Asia in two. In one direction it faces the sea that washes Cilicia, in another the Caspian, the river Araxes and also the desert areas of Scythia. The Taurus range, which is of lesser height, joins the Caucasus, rising in Cappadocia, skirting Cilicia and merging into the mountains of Armenia. Thus interconnected in a series, these ranges form an unbroken chain, which is the source for practically all the rivers of Asia, some flowing into the Red, some into the Caspian, and others into the Hyrcanian and Pontic seas. The army crossed the Caucasus in seventeen days. According to ancient tradition, it was on a rocky crag in this chain – one with a perimeter of ten stades and a height of four – that Prometheus was bound. The foot of this mountain was selected as a site for building a city, and permission to settle in the new town was granted to 7,000 of the older Macedonians as well as to other soldiers retired by Alexander. This, too, was called Alexandria by its inhabitants.

Bessus was terrified by Alexander's speed. He had made due sacrifice to the local gods and, after the practice of those races, was holding a council of war with his friends and officers over a banquet. Sodden with drink, they began to flatter themselves on their strength and to make disparaging remarks about both the overconfidence and the numerical weakness of the enemy. Bessus was especially boastful in his language; his arrogance after treacherously usurping his throne bordered on madness. He began to claim that it was Darius' negligence that had increased the enemy's reputation, that he had faced them in the narrowest defiles of Cilicia when retreat would have enabled him to lead them on into naturally protected areas without their realizing it. There were so many rivers to serve as obstacles and so many hiding places in the mountains, he said; caught among these, the enemy would have had no chance to escape, much less offer resistance. His decision now, he declared, was to draw back into the territory of the Sogdians and to use the river Oxus as a barrier against the enemy until strong reinforcements could amalgamate from the neighbouring tribes. The Chorasmians would come, and so would the Dahae, the Sacae, the Indians and the Scythians living beyond the river Tanais – and not a man among these was so short that his shoulders could not stand level with a Macedonian soldier's head! His drunken friends all shouted out that this was the only sound idea, and Bessus ordered more generous helpings of neat wine to be carried around as he planned his defeat of Alexander at the dinner table. (Curtius)

Bessus had an army of 8,000 Bactrians who faithfully carried out his orders as long as they thought their intemperate climate would make the Macedonians head for India but, when it was discovered that Alexander was approaching, they all slipped off to their villages and abandoned him. With a group of dependants who had not changed their allegiance, he crossed the river Oxus, burned the boats used for crossing to stop the enemy using them, and started levying fresh troops among the Sogdians.

Alexander had already crossed the Caucasus, as was related above, but grain shortages had brought the troops to the verge of starvation. The men rubbed their bodies with juice from pressed sesame in lieu of oil, though the cost of this juice was 240 denarii per jar, and honey and wine respectively cost 390 and 300 denarii. As for wheat, there was none, or very little, to be found. (Their crops were hidden by the barbarians in what they called *siri*, so cunningly concealed that only the men who dug them could find them.) Lacking such provisions, the men survived on fresh-water fish and herbs and, when even those means of sustenance had run out, they were given orders to slaughter the pack animals. They managed to stay alive on the meat from these until they reached the Bactrians. (Curtius)

Entrusting Bactria to Artabazus, Alexander left his baggage and equipment there under guard while he entered the desert areas of Sogdiana with a light-armed force, leading the troops by night. The lack of water, mentioned above, was such that desperation produced a parching thirst even before a natural craving to drink appeared. For 400 stades no trace of water was to be found. The heat of the summer sun scorched the sands and, when these started to heat up, everything on them was baked as if by perpetual fire. Then a misty vapour thrown up by the burning heat of the earth obscured the daylight, giving the plains the appearance of one vast, deep ocean. Travel by night seemed bearable because dew and the early morning freshness would bring relief to their bodies; but with the dawn came the heat, draining with its aridity all natural moisture and deeply burning the mouth and the stomach. So it was their resolution that failed first, and then their bodies. They were unwilling to stop and unwilling to go on. A few had followed the advice of people who knew the country and stored up some water. This slaked their thirst for a short time, but then the increasing heat re-kindled their craving for water. Consequently all the wine and oil in anyone's possession was consumed, too, and such was the pleasure they gained from drinking it that they had no fear of thirst in the future. Subsequently the liquid they had greedily drained put such a weight on their stomachs that they could neither hold up their weapons nor continue their journey, and the men who had been without water now seemed to be more fortunate than they themselves, since they were forced to spew up the water they had immoderately consumed.

These urgent problems distressed Alexander. His friends stood around him and begged him to remember that his intrepid spirit was all that could restore the fortunes of his languishing army. At this point he was met by two of the men who had gone ahead to select a camp site. They were carrying skins of water to bring relief to their sons who, they knew, were suffering from severe thirst in Alexander's column. On meeting the king one of them opened a skin, filled a cup he was carrying, and offered it to him. Alexander took it. Then he asked for whom they were carrying the water and learned it was for their sons. He returned the cup, as full as when it was offered to him, saying, 'I cannot bear to drink alone and it is not possible for me to share so little with everybody. Go quickly and give your sons what you have brought on their account.'

Finally, around early evening, Alexander reached the river Oxus, but most of the troops had been unable to keep pace with him. He had beacons lit on a mountain peak so that men having difficulty keeping up could see they were not far from camp. Those at the front of the column, quickly revived by something to eat and drink, were ordered by Alexander to fill skins, or any vessels that could serve for carrying water, and to bring relief to their comrades. But some men gulped the water down too greedily and died from blockage of the windpipe – and the number of these exceeded the numbers Alexander had lost in any battle. As for the king, he stood at the point where the troops were arriving, still wearing his cuirass and without having taken any food or drink, and he did not leave to take refreshment until the entire column had passed him. All night through after that he remained sleepless, his mind deeply troubled. The next day he was no happier. He had no boats, and constructing a bridge was ruled out by the barrenness of the land around the river and specifically by the absence of wood. Accordingly he embarked on the only plan suggested to him by the exigencies of this situation, and distributed to the men, in numbers as great as was possible, skins stuffed with straw. Lying on these the men swam the river, and those first over stood on guard for the others to cross. In this way Alexander deposited the entire army on the far bank in five days.

After deciding to proceed in pursuit of Bessus, he learned of the situation in Sogdiana. Among all Bessus' friends Spitamenes enjoyed a special position of honour – but no benefactions can serve to palliate treachery (though in this case it might have earned less disapproval because no one would regard as abominable any act against Bessus, who had murdered his own king). Spitamenes' coup even had a specious pretext, namely vengeance for Darius, but it was Bessus' success, not his crime, that had aroused his hatred. On learning that Alexander had crossed the river Oxus, Spitamenes enlisted as associates in his plot Dataphernes and Catanes, who enjoyed Bessus' highest confidence. They were no sooner asked than they gave their support. Taking with them eight sturdy young men, they set the following trap. Spitamenes went to Bessus and in strict privacy told him that he had discovered a plot against him by Dataphernes and Catanes, that these planned to deliver him alive into Alexander's hands. He, however, had anticipated their move and was holding them in custody.

Bessus, believing himself under obligation for this great favour, thanked Spitamenes and at the same time, impatient to punish the culprits, had them brought to him. These had agreed to have their hands tied up and were now dragged in by their fellow conspirators. Bessus gave them a savage look and rose to his feet, unable to keep his hands off them. But the conspirators dropped their pretence, encircled him and, while he vainly tried to resist, tied him up, pulling from his head the royal diadem and ripping off the clothes he had assumed from the spoils of his dead king. The gods, Bessus admitted, had come to exact vengeance for his crime; but they had not been unfavourable to Darius whom they avenged, but propitious to Alexander, who had always enjoyed even his enemy's help to win a victory. Whether the barbarian masses would have freed Bessus is debatable, but the man who had tied him up frightened those still wavering by falsely claiming that they had acted on Alexander's orders. They put Bessus on a horse and led him away to surrender him to Alexander.

Meanwhile the king selected some 900 men due for discharge and made them gifts of two talents per cavalryman and 3,000 denarii per infantryman. These he sent home with instructions to produce children. The other troops were thanked for their promise of support for the remainder of the campaign.

In pursuit of Bessus they had arrived at a small town inhabited by the Branchidae who, on the orders of Xerxes when he was returning from Greece, had emigrated from Miletus and settled in this spot. This was necessary because, to please Xerxes, they had violated the temple called the Didymeon. The culture of their forebears had not yet disappeared, though they were by now bilingual and the foreign tongue was gradually eroding their own. So it was with great joy that they welcomed Alexander, to whom they surrendered themselves and their city. Alexander called a meeting of the Milesians in his force, for the Milesians bore a long-standing grudge against the Branchidae as a clan. Since they were the people betrayed by the Branchidae, Alexander let them decide freely on their case, asking if they preferred to remember their injury or their common origin. But when there was a difference of opinion over this, he declared that he would himself consider the best course of action.

When the Branchidae met him the next day, he told them to accompany him. On reaching the city, he himself entered through the gate with a unit of light-armed troops. The phalanx had been ordered to surround the city walls and, when the signal was given, to sack this city which provided refuge for traitors, killing the inhabitants to a man. The Branchidae, who were unarmed, were butchered throughout the city, and neither community of language nor the olive branches and entreaties of the suppliants could curb the savagery. Finally the Macedonians dug down to the foundations of the walls in order to demolish them and leave not a single trace of the city. Woods, too, and sacred groves, they not only cut down but actually uprooted, so that nothing would remain after the removal of the roots but empty wasteland and barren soil. Had this punishment been devised against the people responsible for the treachery, it might have appeared to be fair revenge rather than brutality but, as it was, the guilt of their ancestors was being atoned for by descendants who had not even seen Miletus and accordingly could not possibly have betrayed it to Xerxes.

Alexander advanced from there to the river Tanais, where Bessus was brought to him, not only in irons but entirely stripped of his clothes. Spitamenes held him with a chain around his neck, a sight that afforded as much pleasure to the barbarians as to the Macedonians. 'I have avenged both you and Darius, my two sovereigns,' said Spitamenes. 'I have brought you the man who killed his master, after capturing him in a manner for which he himself set the precedent. I wish Darius could open his eyes to see this spectacle! I wish he could rise from the dead – he ill deserved such an end and well deserves this consolation!'

Alexander bestowed enthusiastic praise on Spitamenes and then turned to Bessus. 'What bestial madness possessed you,' he said, 'that you should dare to imprison and then murder a king from whom you had received exemplary treatment? Yes, and you rewarded yourself for this treachery with the title of king which was not yours.' Bessus dared not make excuses for his crime. He claimed that he adopted the title of king so that he could surrender his country to Alexander, and failure to do so would have resulted in another seizing the throne.

Alexander told Darius' brother Oxathres (who was one of his bodyguards) to approach him, and had Bessus put in his charge. Bessus was to be hung on a cross, his ears and nose cut off, and the barbarians were to shoot arrows into him and also protect his body from the carrion birds. Oxathres promised to take care of everything, but added that the birds could be kept off only by Catanes, whose superb workmanship Oxathres wished to put on display. Catanes, in fact, was so accurate in hitting what he aimed at that he could even pick off birds. These days, when archery is a widespread practice, this expertise of his might seem less remarkable; but at that time spectators found it an absolutely amazing phenomenon and Catanes won great respect. Gifts were then awarded by Alexander to all responsible for bringing in Bessus, but his execution he postponed so that he could be killed in the very spot where he had himself murdered Darius.

Meanwhile a group of Macedonians had gone off to forage out of formation and were surprised by some barbarians who came rushing down on them from the neighbouring mountains. More were taken prisoner than were killed, and the barbarians retired once more to the high ground, driving their captives before them. These bandits numbered 20,000, and the weapons they used in combat were slings and arrows. Alexander laid siege to them and, while he fought in the forefront of the battle, he was hit by an arrow, the head of which was left firmly lodged in his leg. Dismayed and alarmed, the Macedonians carried him back to camp.

The barbarians were also aware that he had been removed from the fight, since they had a full view of the conflict from their high position on the mountain. So the next day they dispatched an embassy to the king, which Alexander ordered be given an immediate audience. Then, unwinding his bandages but concealing the extent of his wound, he showed the barbarians his leg. After they were told to be seated, the envoys declared that the Macedonians were no more saddened at the news of the king's wound than they were themselves and, if they had found the culprit, they would already have surrendered him, since it was only the sacrilegious who fought against gods. Furthermore, they continued, they had now because of his wound been constrained to surrender to him. Alexander gave them assurances, took back the Macedonian prisoners, and accepted their surrender.

After this he moved camp, and was carried on a military litter, but who should carry this was disputed by the cavalry and the infantry. The cavalry, with whom the king usually went into battle, thought it was their prerogative, while the infantry, since it had been usual for them to carry their wounded comrades, kept complaining that a job that was rightfully theirs was being filched from them just at the time when it was the king who needed carrying. Since the quarrel between the two sides was so acrimonious, and the choice both difficult for him to make and sure to cause offence to the losers, the king ordered them to take turns in carrying him. (Curtius)

*

A few days later, envoys came to Alexander from the people known as the Abian Scythians. (These are the people whom Homer praises in his epic, calling them the most righteous of men. They live in Asia and are independent, largely because of their poverty and just behaviour.) He also received envoys from the European Scythians, the largest tribe living in Europe. Alexander sent back some of the Companions with them, purportedly as ambassadors to arrange some alliance, but intending, in fact, that they should ascertain the nature of the Scythians' territory, their numbers, their customs, and whatever arms they had at their disposal for military expeditions.

Alexander had it in mind to found a city named after himself on the river Tanais. The site seemed to offer potential for continuing expansion and the city would also be built in a good position, both for invading Scythia (if he went ahead with this), and for guarding the region against attacks by the tribesmen who dwelt on the other side of the river. He envisaged that the number of settlers, together with the glory of his name, would ensure the greatness of this city.

However, the tribesmen who lived by the river now seized and slew the Macedonian soldiers who were posted as guards in their cities and started to build up even stronger defences. Many of the people of Sogdiana joined their uprising, spurred on by the group who had arrested Bessus, with the consequence that some of the Bactrians were also drawn into the revolt. The cause of the revolt may possibly have been fear of Alexander; or it may be that these men rebelled because Alexander had called for a meeting of the native leaders at the capital Zariaspa, and they were suspicious of his motives.

Alexander responded to the news of the revolt by ordering every section of the infantry to make a certain number of scaling ladders, while he himself set off towards Gaza,* the town nearest to his camp; he had heard that the natives of this region had gathered together in seven such towns. Craterus was dispatched to Cyropolis, the largest of them, where the biggest group of tribesmen was to be found. He had been given orders to set up

* The Sogdian, as opposed to the Phoenician, Gaza.

camp near the town, dig a ditch around it, and surround it with a stockade. He was then to assemble as many siege engines as necessary, so that the people within the city, directing their full attention towards his forces, would be unable to come to the aid of their allies. (Arrian)

Alexander then suppresses the rebellion throughout the region.

Once these affairs were settled, Alexander arrived at Zariaspa and stayed there through the worst of the winter. While he was there, Phrataphernes, satrap of Parthia, and Stasanor, who had been sent to Aria to arrest Arsaces, arrived with Arsaces in chains, along with Barzanes, who had once been appointed satrap of Parthia by Bessus, and some of the others who had joined in Bessus' revolt. Also at this time there arrived from the coast Epocillus, Menidas and Ptolemaeus, the Thracian general, who had just escorted the treasures sent with Menes and the allies to the sea; Asander and Nearchus, leading a Greek mercenary force; and another Bessus, the satrap of Syria, with Asclepiodorus, his second-in-command, bringing their soldiers with them.

Alexander called everyone to a meeting and led Bessus out before them, accusing him of treachery to Darius. He gave orders that Bessus' nose, along with the tips of his ears, should be cut off and that Bessus should then be taken to Ectabana, to be executed before an assembly of Medes and Persians. (Arrian)

Now seems a good point to relate the death of Cleitus and Alexander's subsequent suffering, although this affair actually happened a little later. Among the Macedonians took place once a year a festival in honour of Dionysus, at which Alexander used to make a sacrifice to the god. It is reported, however, that on one occasion Alexander neglected to do so, deciding, for an unknown reason, to sacrifice to the Dioscuri* instead. By then Alexander had already adopted barbarian drinking customs, and the drinking during the celebrations was getting progress-

---

* The heavenly twins, Castor and Pollux.

ively heavier when the conversation turned to the matter of the Dioscuri and the common belief that Zeus, rather than Tyndareus, was their father. Some of the people there – the type of men who bring corruption and are a constant source of weakness in royal affairs – flattered their king by claiming that the achievements of Castor and Pollux could not even be compared to those of Alexander, while others, drunk as they were, went so far as to say the same of Hercules. Envy alone, they said, hindered the living from being rightfully honoured by their companions.

Yet Cleitus was clearly troubled by Alexander's shift towards barbarian ways and by the words of his flatterers. Now, spurred on by the wine, he could no longer tolerate such dishonouring of divine beings or belittling of ancient heroic deeds, this favouring of Alexander which in fact did him no favours. According to Cleitus, neither the scale nor the marvel of Alexander's achievements merited such exaltation. Moreover, they were, for the most part, Macedonian achievements and not his alone.

Cleitus' words were deeply upsetting to Alexander – and I do not think that he was right to say them; amid such drunkenness, it would have been easy enough for him to eschew the foolish flattery of the others by keeping his thoughts to himself. But then, some of the men turned to the deeds of Philip and, in an attempt to flatter Alexander further, made the utterly unjust claims that Philip had achieved nothing great or remarkable. At this, Cleitus lost all control and praised Philip's achievements, while denigrating Alexander and his actions. In fact, Cleitus was so drunk by now that he admonished Alexander severely, boasting that he was himself responsible for saving Alexander when they had fought against the Persian cavalry at the Granicus. His ultimate insult was to raise his right hand, as he declared, 'This is the very hand which saved you then!'

No longer able to bear Cleitus' drunken insolence, Alexander threw himself at him, furious, only to be restrained by his fellow drinkers. Yet Cleitus went on with his insults. Alexander shouted out, calling on the Guards, but no one responded. This led Alexander to exclaim that his predicament now matched that of Darius, taken prisoner by Bessus and his men; he was king by name alone.

Now his friends could hold him back no longer. Leaping up, some say he grabbed a spear from one of his bodyguards and used it to kill Cleitus. Others claim that he used a pike. Aristobulus does not go into what caused the drunken brawl, but he does lay all the blame on Cleitus, saying that as the enraged Alexander leapt up to kill him, Ptolemy, son of Lagus, and one of the bodyguards took Cleitus outside through the doors and over the wall and the ditch of the citadel. However, even then, Cleitus did not restrain himself, but turned round and went straight back to Alexander, just as the latter called out his name. It was Cleitus' response, 'Here is your Cleitus, Alexander', which drove Alexander to kill him with a blow from a pike.

For my part, I very much hold Cleitus to blame for such insults against his own king; whereas I pity Alexander, who is shown here to have fallen prey to two faults, fury and drunkenness, neither of which becomes a prudent man. In terms of the events that followed, I do, however, praise Alexander for recognizing immediately that he had done a terrible thing. Some say that Alexander stood the pike against the wall with the intention of throwing himself upon it. Having killed his own friend out of drunkenness, he no longer felt himself worthy of life. However, most writers do not mention this episode; they report that he took to his bed, wailing, shouting out the name of Cleitus and of his nurse, Cleitus' sister, the daughter of Dropides. 'Now that I am grown to manhood,' he cried, 'what fine reward I have given you for rearing me, you who have witnessed your very own sons dying in battle on my behalf! For I, with my very own hand, have slain your brother.' Denouncing himself without cease as the murderer of his friends, he abstained from food, drink and all other bodily needs for three whole days. (Arrian)

While Alexander was occupied with such matters, Spitamenes, along with some of the fugitives from Sogdiana, had fled to the country of those Scythians known as the Massagetae, where they gathered together 600 horsemen from among the local population, before coming to one of the Bactrian forts. Here they attacked the commander, who was not expecting any hostilities, along with the men who had been keeping guard under his command. They killed the soldiers, but captured and held their leader. Emboldened by the capture of this guardpost, they approached Zariaspa a few days later, but decided against attacking the city, instead seizing many heads of cattle as booty.

In Zariaspa remained a few of the Companion cavalry who had been left behind because of illness, including Peitho, son of Sosicles, appointed as royal attendant, and Aristonicus, the harpist. These men were now well enough to bear arms and mount their horses. So, when they learnt about the Scythian raid, they gathered together about eighty of the mercenary cavalry who were guarding Zariaspa and some of the royal squires and rode out against the Massagetae. The first wave of their attack took the Scythians by surprise and led to the recapturing of the booty and the killing of many of those who were driving it away. Yet, with no one to lead their disorderly retreat, the attackers were ambushed by Spitamenes and the Scythians, losing seven of the Companions and sixty of the mercenary cavalry. Aristonicus died on the spot, acting as a man of courage rather than a mere harpist, while Peitho was wounded and taken by the Scythians.

When the news reached Craterus he advanced at full speed against the Massagetae, who fled into the desert as fast they could as soon as they heard of his approach. Craterus closed in on them near the desert and attacked them, as well as a force of over 1,000 Massagataean horsemen. A mighty battle ensued between the Macedonians and the Scythians, in which the Macedonians were victorious; 150 Scythians were killed, while the rest made an easy escape into the desert, where further Macedonian pursuit would have proved too difficult.

Meanwhile Alexander had granted Artabazus' request to be released from the satrapy of Bactria on account of his old age, and appointed Amyntas, son of Nicolaus, in his place. He left Coenus there with his own and Meleager's battalions, as well as around 400 of the Companion cavalry, all the mounted javelin men, and all of the Bactrians and Sogdians who had been posted with Amyntas. The orders were that the entire force led by Coenus was to remain for the winter in Sogdiana, to keep watch over this territory, and to see whether they could apprehend Spitamenes in an ambush, should he venture that way.

When Spitamenes and his men saw that all positions were guarded by the Macedonians and every means of escape barred, they marched against Coenus and his army, deciding that this might ensure them a more even battle. On their arrival in Bagae, a Sogdian stronghold that lies between the lands of the Sogdian and the Massagetaean Scythians, they found it easy to persuade some 3,000 Scythian horsemen to join them in their attack on Sogdiana. Extreme poverty, combined with the absence of cities and a lack of fixed homes, means that these Scythians have no dearest possessions for which to fear, and are easily led into any war that arises.

As soon as Coenus and his men learnt that Spitamenes was approaching with his cavalry, they went out to meet him. The Macedonians were victorious in the great battle which now took place: the casualties amounted to over 800 of enemy cavalry, but only around twenty-five cavalry and twelve infantry from among Coenus' men. The remaining Sogdians, together with the majority of the Bactrians, deserted Spitamenes as he fled and came to Coenus in order to give themselves up; for their part, the Massagetaean Scythians reacted to this disaster by plundering the baggage-trains of the very Bactrians and Sogdians alongside whom they had fought, before retreating into the desert with Spitamenes. Finally, when they learnt that Alexander was now heading into the desert towards them, they cut off Spitamenes' head and sent it to him, hoping that this action might protect them from him. (Arrian)

At the first signs of spring, Alexander set off for the Rock of Sogdiana where, he was told, many of the Sogdians had fled, including the wife and children of Oxyartes, the Bactrian who had revolted against Alexander, and who had secretly sent his family to the Rock in the belief that such a place was unconquerable. If the Rock were to be captured, any aspiring rebel from Sogdiana would be left without hope.

As they approached the Rock, the Macedonians did find that every aspect of it rose steeply up against attack, while the enemy had laid in sufficient provisions for a long siege and had been furnished with a plentiful supply of water by the thick snow that had fallen on the summit, which also increased the difficulty of ascent for the Macedonians. Still, Alexander was determined to launch an assault as a point of honour, angered by some offensive and arrogant remark made by the tribesmen. They had been summoned to a meeting at which he had offered them the chance to return safely to their homes, provided that they surrender the fortress. Responding with barbaric laughter, they told Alexander he should search for the winged soldiers who might capture the mountain for him, since they had no concern for other kinds of men. At this, Alexander declared a prize of twelve talents for the first to ascend the mountain, eleven for the second, ten for the third, and so on up to the twelfth, whose prize would be 300 darics.* The Macedonians, already eager, were spurred on more than ever by his pronouncement.

Roughly 300 men gathered – all those had practised rock-climbing during previous sieges. They had brought the small iron pegs used for securing their tents, which they could push into any patch of snow that was frozen solid or any bit of dry ground they might come across, and they had tied the pegs together with strong flaxen ropes. They set off by night to the steepest and therefore least well-guarded part of the rock. Driving their pegs into any patch of earth they could find or into the bits of snow they thought least likely to give way they hauled themselves up as best they could on to the rock. The thirty men who died during the ascent fell into the snow in different places, and it was impossible to find the bodies for burial. The remainder, however, made it to the top at daybreak and captured the summit of the mountain, waving to the Macedonian camp with linen flags, as Alexander had instructed. At this, Alexander dispatched a herald to proclaim to the enemy's advance guard that it was now time for them to surrender without further delay, for he had found his winged men and the summit of the

* The equivalent of one talent.

rock was in their possession. He accompanied the proclamation by pointing to his soldiers on the summit.

At such unexpected sight the tribesmen were thrown into a panic and, believing that a large and well-armed force now held the summit, they surrendered themselves on account of the fear inspired by those few Macedonians they could see. Many of their women and children were captured, including the wife and children of Oxyartes. Now Oxyartes had a daughter of marriageable age called Roxane, who those who had fought with Alexander declared to be the most beautiful women in all Asia, except for the wife of Darius. For Alexander, it was love at first sight. Though he loved her, he refused to take advantage of her being his prisoner and deigned, instead, to marry her. (Arrian)

The marriage takes place after the capture of the neighbouring rock fortress of Sisimithres. It is also around this time that the Callisthenes affair takes place.

According to Hermippus, this is the account which Stroebus, the slave who read aloud for Callisthenes, gave to Aristotle of the quarrel between Callisthenes and Alexander. He also says that when Callisthenes understood that he had antagonized the king, he repeated two or three times, as he was taking his leave, this verse from the *Iliad*

Braver by far than yourself was Patroclus, but death did not spare him.

Aristotle seems to have come near the truth when he said that Callisthenes possessed great eloquence, but lacked common sense. But at least in the matter of the obeisance he behaved like a true philosopher, not only in his sturdy refusal to perform it, but also in being the only man to express in public the resentment which all the oldest and best of the Macedonians felt in private. By persuading the king not to insist on this tribute, he delivered the Greeks from a great disgrace and Alexander from an even greater one, but at the same time he destroyed himself, because he left the impression that he had gained his point by force rather than by persuasion.

Chares of Mitylene says that on one occasion at a banquet Alexander, after he had drunk, passed the cup to one of his friends, who took it and rose so as to face the shrine of the household; next he drank in his turn, then made obeisance to Alexander, kissed him and resumed his place on the couch. All the guests did the same in succession, until the cup came to Callisthenes. The king was talking to Hephaestion and paying no attention to Callisthenes, and the philosopher, after he had drunk, came forward to kiss him. At this Demetrius, whose surname was Pheido, called out, 'Sire, do not kiss him; he is the only one who has not made obeisance to you.' Alexander therefore refused to kiss him, and Callisthenes exclaimed in a loud voice, 'Very well then, I shall go away the poorer by a kiss.' (Plutarch)

Curtius' view of Callisthenes' death is heavily biased against Alexander, but is only one of several conflicting accounts.

In the case of Callisthenes, whom he had long suspected because of his outspokenness, his resentment was more persistent. An opportunity to indulge this soon came his way. It was customary for the Macedonian nobility to deliver their grown-up sons to their kings for the performance of duties which differed little from the tasks of slaves. They would take turns spending the night on guard at the door of the king's bedchamber, and it was they who brought in his women by an entrance other than that watched by the armed guards. They would also take his horses from the grooms and bring them for him to mount; they were his attendants both on the hunt and in battle, and were highly educated in all the liberal arts. It was thought a special honour that they were allowed to sit and eat with the king. No one had the authority to flog them apart from the king himself. This company served the Macedonians as a kind of seminary for their officers and generals, and from it subsequently came the kings whose descendants were many generations later stripped of power by the Romans.

Now Hermolaus was a young nobleman who belonged to the group of royal attendants. He was flogged on Alexander's orders for having speared a boar before the king when the latter had ear-marked it for himself. Stung by this humiliation, he began to complain to Sostratus, who also belonged to the group and was passionately in love with Hermolaus. Sostratus now saw the lacerations on the body he desperately loved, and it is possible that he bore the king some other grudge from the past. So, after the two had exchanged oaths of loyalty, Sostratus prevailed on the boy, who was already so inclined on his own account, to enter into a plot with him to assassinate the king. Nor was it with the impulsiveness of youth that they put their plan into action, for they were discreet in selecting the people they would invite to join the conspiracy. They decided that Nicostratus, Antipater, Asclepiodorus and Philotas should be enlisted, and through these Anticles, Elaptonius and Epimenes were also brought in. However, no easy method of executing the plan presented itself. It was imperative that all the conspirators be on guard duty the same night, so that there should be no problem with people not party to the plot, but it turned out that they were all on duty on different nights. As a result, thirty-two days were taken up with altering the rota for guard duty and other preparations for executing the plot.

It was now the night on which the conspirators were to be on duty. They were cheered by their unanimous commitment to the cause, demonstrated by the number of days that had gone by during which none had wavered through fear or hope – so strong was their common resentment towards Alexander or their loyalty to each other. They now stood at the door of the room in which the king was dining, intending to escort him to his bedroom when he left the banquet. But Alexander's good fortune, plus the conviviality of the banqueters, led the company to drink more than usual, and the dinner-party games also drew out the time, which made the conspirators alternately happy at the prospect of falling on a drowsy victim and anxious that he might prolong the party till daylight. The problem was that others were due to relieve them at dawn, their turn of duty would not recur for seven days and they could not expect the discretion of all of them to last till that time.

At the approach of dawn, however, the banquet broke up and the conspirators received the king, pleased that an opportunity for executing the crime had arrived. Then a woman appeared who, it as thought, was out of her senses and who used to frequent the royal quarters (for she appeared inspired and able to foretell the future). She did not only meet the king as he took his leave but actually threw herself in his path. Her facial expression and her eyes indicating some inner agitation, she warned him to return to the banquet. By way of a joke Alexander answered that the gods gave good advice. He once more summoned his friends and prolonged the banquet until almost the second hour of the day.

By now other members of the group of attendants had succeeded to their positions and were ready to stand guard before Alexander's bedroom door, but the conspirators kept standing around even though their turn on duty was completed; so long-lived is hope once the human mind has seized upon it. Addressing them more warmly than usual, the king told them to go and rest since they had been on their feet all night. They were given fifty sesterces each and commended for remaining on duty even when the turn of others had come. Their great hope frustrated, they went home. They now began to wait for their next night on duty, all except Epimenes, who experienced a sudden change of heart, either because of the friendly manner in which the king had greeted him and the other conspirators or because he believed that the gods opposed their scheme. So he revealed what was afoot to his brother Eurylochus, whom he had previously wished to remain ignorant of the plot.

The spectre of Philotas' punishment was hanging before everybody's eyes. Eurylochus accordingly seized his brother immediately and came with him into the royal quarters. He alerted the bodyguards and declared that the information he brought related to the king's security. The time of their coming and the expressions on their faces, revealing obviously troubled minds, plus the dejection of one of them – all this alarmed Ptolemy and Leonnatus, who were standing guard at the bedroom door. They opened the door, took in a lamp and woke Alexander, who now lay in a deep, drunken sleep. Gradually coming to his senses, he asked what news they brought. Without a moment's hesitation Eurylochus asserted that the gods could not have entirely abandoned his family because his brother, although he had embarked on an impious crime, now regretted his actions and wished no one but himself to bring information about the plot to Alexander. The coup, he said, had been planned for that very night which was now passing, and those responsible for the heinous plot were men the king would least suspect.

Epimenes then gave a detailed and systematic account, including the names of the conspirators. Callisthenes was certainly not named as one involved in the plot, and it did come out that he was in the habit of giving a ready ear to the talk of the pages when they were criticizing and finding fault with the king. Some people also assert that, when Hermolaus complained before Callisthenes of having been flogged by Alexander, Callisthenes commented that they ought to remember that they were men; but they add that it is unclear whether this remark was meant to comfort Hermolaus after his beating or to provoke resentment in the young men.

Shaking the drowsiness from mind and body, Alexander saw before his eyes the great danger he had escaped. He immediately gave Eurylochus fifty talents, plus the rich property of a certain Tyridates, and he restored his brother to him even before Eurylochus could beg for his life. The culprits – and Callisthenes was included – he ordered to be kept in chains. They were brought to the royal quarters, but Alexander was tired from the drink and lack of sleep, and so he slept throughout the day and the next night. The day after that, however, he convened a general assembly. This was attended by the fathers and relatives of the accused, not free of concern for their own safety in view of the Macedonian custom which required their death, since all blood relations of the guilty party were liable to execution. Alexander had all the conspirators apart from Callisthenes brought in, and without hesitation they confessed their plan. There was a general outcry against them, and the king himself asked what he had done to merit their hatching such a wicked plot against him. (Curtius)

Alexander rejects Hermolaus' defence of his actions.

With that Alexander closed the meeting and had the condemned men transferred to members of their own unit. The latter tortured them to death so that they would gain the king's approval by their cruelty. Callisthenes also died under torture. He was innocent of any plot to kill the king, but the sycophantic character of court life ill-suited his nature. As a result no other person's execution engendered greater resentment against Alexander among the Greeks. Callisthenes was a man of the finest character and accomplishments who had restored Alexander to life when he was determined to die after the murder of Cleitus. Alexander had not merely executed him but had tortured him as well – and without trial. This barbarous act was, all too late, followed by feelings of remorse. (Curtius)

7. EAST INTO INDIA – THE UNCOMPLETED CAMPAIGN

In summer 327 Alexander leaves Bactra and crosses the Hindu Kush once again. Guided by the rajah Sasigupta, he makes his way into India, suppressing any local resistance. Eventually he pushes his Indian opponents back to the rock fortress at Aornos, which he manages to storm, in spite of the difficulties. He moves on to Taxila, but leaves in May 326, heading for the Indus. After a significant victory at the Jhelum river he allows the defeated Porus to keep his kingdom, and founds two cities, one named after his horse Bucephalus, who dies at Jhelum. Before setting off across the Punjab, Alexander worships the sun and gives orders for a fleet to be built, believing that the Indus flows into the Nile and will later provide a direct route home. He then marches along the river Acesines (Chenab), subjugating numerous towns along his way, but is plagued by floods and snakes as late summer brings the monsoons. The Acesines is crossed with difficulty and, after wading across the river Hydraotes (Ravi), the army wins a huge victory against the Cathaioi on the plains near Sangala (Lahore or Amritsar). Across the Hyphasis (Beas), the last of the Punjab's rivers, is the kingdom which surrounds the Ganges, the final part of India remaining to be conquered. Yet, even though Alexander is advised that these lands are rich and that victory should be within his grasp, his men are exhausted, their spirits broken at last by the hardships of the monsoon. Led by Coenus, an old and respected general, they refuse to continue. Having come so close to complete domination of India, Alexander is forced to give in to his men and begins his retreat.

After entering the boundaries of India, Alexander was met by the petty kings of the area, who were prepared to submit to his authority. He was, they said, the third son of Jupiter to have reached them but, whereas they knew of Father Liber and Hercules only by report, Alexander had come in person and was before their eyes. The king gave them a courteous welcome and instructed them to accompany him, for he intended using them as guides for his journeys. When no one else came to meet him, he sent Hephaestion and Perdiccas ahead with a section of his troops to crush any opposition to his power, giving them orders to advance to the river Indus and construct boats to ferry the army to the far banks. Because a number of rivers had to be crossed, they put the boats together in such a way that they could be dismantled, transported by wagon and then reassembled.

Alexander instructed Craterus to follow him with the phalanx, and then led out his cavalry and light-armed infantry. After a slight skirmish with some Indians who confronted him, he drove them into the nearest city. By this time Craterus had arrived and so, to strike terror right at the start into a people which had, as yet, had no experience of Macedonian arms, he told him to show no mercy after the fortifications of the city under siege had been fired. Riding up to the walls, however, Alexander was hit by an arrow, despite which he took the town, butchered its inhabitants to a man, and even unleashed his fury on its buildings.

Next, after subduing some tribe of little account, he came to the city of Nysa. It so happened that after he had pitched camp in a wooded spot right before the walls, there was an unprecedented drop in temperature during the night which made the men shiver with cold. A fire offered itself as a convenient remedy. Cutting down some trees, they started a blaze, but this, fuelled by the logs, engulfed the sepulchres of the townspeople. The sepulchres had been made of old cedar which, once they had caught fire, spread the flames over a wide area until they were all razed to the ground. From the city came the sound first of dogs barking, then of men in an uproar, and it was at this point that the townspeople realized that their enemy had reached their city and the Macedonians that they had arrived.

After Alexander had led out his troops and was laying siege to the walls, a number of the enemy attempted a sortie, only to fall beneath a barrage of missiles. Accordingly, some of the inhabitants advocated surrender, while others were for risking a battle. When Alexander learned that they were hesitating, he ordered a blockade but no bloodshed. Worn down by the difficulties of the siege, the enemy finally capitulated. (Curtius)

On his way to Aornos, Alexander first marched to the river Indus, taking control peacefully of Peucelaotis, a town situated near the Indus, where he set up a garrison of Macedonians under the command of Philip. He also took over a number of small towns along the river, accompanied on his march by the local chieftains Cophaeus and Assagetes. When he arrived at the town of Embolima, which lies near the rock of Aornos, he left Craterus behind with part of the army, so that they could bring as much food as possible into the city as well as all other essentials for a lengthy stay. This would allow the Macedonians to use the town as a base for a long siege and wear away at the occupying forces on the rock, if it could not be taken in an attack. Meanwhile Alexander himself approached the rock, taking with him the archers, the Agrianes, Coenus' division and a select group of the lightest but best-armed men from the other phalanx, around 200 of the Companion cavalry and 100 mounted archers. On this day he camped in what appeared to be the most convenient spot, but he then moved on a little way towards the rock the day after and set up camp again.

Meanwhile a group of locals came to Alexander to surrender themselves, claiming that they would lead him to the part of the rock which was most open to attack, from where an easy capture would be assured. Alexander sent his bodyguard, Ptolemy, son of Lagus, with a force comprising Agrianes, the remainder of the light infantry and a select group of Guards, to go along with these men, and gave orders that once they had taken this position, Ptolemy should put in place a strong occupying guard and signal his success to Alexander. In spite of the rough and difficult route, Ptolemy managed to take the position without being seen by the enemy and, having fortified it with a surrounding stockade and trench, he lit a fire-signal on a part of the mountain that would be visible to Alexander. Alexander saw the signal immediately and led forward his army on the following day; no success, however, was achieved, due to enemy resistance and the difficult terrain. When they realized that Alexander's attack had failed, the natives themselves turned on Ptolemy's forces, though Ptolemy managed to defend his position against the Indians' eager attempts to tear down the stockade. Overwhelmed by Macedonian bombardments, the Indians retreated at nightfall.

Alexander now selected one of the Indian deserters, who was not only loyal, but also extremely knowledgeable about the country, and sent him to Ptolemy during the night, carrying a letter with the following instructions: Ptolemy was not to be content with simply maintaining his position, but, as soon as Alexander launched his assault on the rock, he was to attack the enemy from the mountain, so that the Indians would be rendered helpless by the double onslaught. At daybreak, then, Alexander left the camp and led the army up the slope by which Ptolemy had made his secret ascent, thinking that his task would be easier once he had forced his way up to join Ptolemy's men. His plan was a success: until midday a fierce battle raged between the Macedonians, who were making their way up the slope, and the Indians, who were throwing missiles at them as they approached; but the Macedonians kept coming, group upon group, reaching the top and resting in turn, just about managing, as evening came, to get through and join up with Ptolemy. From here the newly combined force launched another attack, this time against the rock itself. However, this attack, which brought a close to the day's actions, was still unsuccessful.

At dawn Alexander ordered every soldier to cut a hundred stakes. Once these were cut, he used them to heap up an enormous mound, extending from the crest of the summit where they had camped to the rock, in the belief that arrows and missiles fired from the siege engines would be able to strike the defenders from this point. Everyone joined in with the task of constructing the mound, while Alexander stood at the side looking on, commending those who were working enthusiastically, but also punishing at once anyone who was slacking.

On the first day the army moved the mound forward about 200 yards, while on the second day the slingers, shooting from the portion of the mound that was already built together with the missiles catapulted from the siege engines, managed to stop the Indians from assaulting the men who were still building the mound; finally, within three days, Alexander had a mound that filled the entire space between the top of the hill and Aornos. Then, on the fourth day, a handful of Macedonians forced their way through to occupy a small hill, its height level with the rock, and Alexander lost no time in extending the mound, so that it would continue all the way to the hill over which these few men had now taken control.

Terrified by the unbelievable boldness of the Macedonians, who had now seized a second height, and by the sight of the now continuous mound, the Indians held off from any further resistance, and sent a herald to Alexander to say that they were prepared to surrender the rock on condition that a treaty was agreed. Their intention was to spend the day discussing the terms of the treaty, then to disperse back to their own peoples during the night. When this plan came to Alexander's knowledge, he actually allowed the Indians time to retreat and remove all of the guards from around the rock. Waiting until the retreat was under way, he took about 700 of the Guards, together with the Royal Guards up to the deserted section of the rock and was himself first to make the ascent, while the Macedonians followed, pulling each other up. At a prearranged signal they now turned on the retreating Indians, killing many of them as they fled; others panicked and jumped to their death from the cliffs.

The rock that Heracles himself had not been able to capture now lay in Alexander's control, and Alexander carried out a sacrifice there, before establishing a garrison, which he entrusted to Sisicottus. Sisicottus was an Indian who had some time ago deserted to Bessus in Bactria, but he had then fought alongside

Alexander when he took control of Bactria, and proved himself to be extremely loyal. (Arrian)

Once he had crossed to the other side of the Indus, Alexander made the customary sacrifice, then left the Indus to arrive in Taxila, a great and prosperous city, which is the largest of those that lie between the Indus and Hydaspes rivers. He received a friendly welcome from Taxiles, the city's governor, and the local Indians, and reciprocated by giving them as much of the neighbouring territory as they asked for. It was here that he was visited by envoys from Abisares, the king of the mountain-dwelling Indians; including his brother and other notables, and by envoys from the local governor, Doxareus, all bringing gifts. At Taxila, too, Alexander offered the customary sacrifices and set up athletic and horse-riding contests. He then appointed Philip, son of Machatas, as satrap over the local Indians, and left behind a garrison, together with any soldier incapacitated through illness, before setting off towards the river Hydaspes.

He had already been informed that Porus was on the opposite bank of the Hydaspes with his entire army, intending either to prevent Alexander's crossing or to attack him should he make the attempt. When Alexander realized that this was his plan, he sent Coenus, son of Polemocrates, back to the river Indus, with orders to dismantle all the boats they had used to cross that river and return with them to the Hydaspes. Accordingly, the boats were taken apart and brought to him; the shorter vessels were divided into two pieces, while the thirty-oared vessels were cut into three, and the sections were then brought by cart to the bank of the Hydaspes. Next, accompanied by the force that he had brought to Taxila as well as 5,000 Indians led by Taxiles and the local leaders, Alexander advanced towards the Hydaspes. (Arrian)

Against the Macedonians Porus had marshalled eighty-five enormously powerful elephants and, behind them, 300 chariots and some 30,000 infantry, including archers (who were equipped with arrows too heavy to be shot effectively). Porus himself rode an elephant which towered above the other beasts. His armour, with its gold and silver inlay, lent distinction to an unusually large physique. His physical strength was matched by his courage, and he possessed as much acumen as could exist among savages. The Macedonians were alarmed not only by the appearance of their foes but also by the size of the river which had to be crossed: four stades wide and with a deep bed that nowhere revealed any shallow areas, this presented the appearance of a vast sea. Nor was the current's force any the less in view of the wide expanse of water; in fact, it rushed ahead as a torrential cataract just as if it had been narrowly constricted by its banks, and waves rebounding at several points indicated the presence of unseen rocks.

The bank supplied an even more terrifying scene, covered as it was with horses and men and, standing among them, those immense bodies with their huge bulk; deliberately goaded, these deafened the ears with their horrendous trumpeting. The combination of the river and the enemy suddenly struck terror into hearts which were generally given to confidence and had often proved themselves in battle; for the Macedonians believed their unstable boats could neither be steered to the bank nor safely landed there.

In mid stream lay a thick cluster of islands. Indians and Macedonians both swam over to these, holding their weapons above their heads, and light skirmishes were in progress on them, with both kings using these small-scale encounters to assess the outcome of the major one. Now in the Macedonian army, Hegesimachus and Nicanor had a reputation for daring and recklessness; they were young noblemen, encouraged by the continuing success of their countrymen to disregard any danger. Led by these two and armed only with lances, the most intrepid of the young Macedonians swam to an island which was occupied by a large body of the enemy and, with nothing more than their enterprise for armour, cut down many of the Indians. To retire with glory was possible – if recklessness when it meets with success could ever know moderation! But while they awaited the approaching enemy with disdainful arrogance, they were encircled by men who had swum over unobserved and fell beneath a shower of missiles hurled at long range. Those escaping the enemy were either swept away by the force of the current or sucked down into whirlpools. The engagement did much to bolster the confidence of Porus, who watched the whole thing from the bank.

Perplexed, Alexander finally devised the following scheme to dupe his enemy. There was in the river an island larger than the others; it was, moreover, wooded and well suited for an ambush. There was also a very deep ravine close to the bank which he himself commanded, and this could conceal not only his infantry but even men on horseback. To distract his enemy's attention from this promising spot, Alexander therefore told Ptolemy to make cavalry manoeuvres with all his squadrons at a point far from the island and to strike fear into the Indians at regular intervals by shouting as if he were going to swim across the river. Ptolemy did this for several days, and by this stratagem he also made Porus concentrate his forces in the area he was pretending to attack.

By now the island was out of the enemy's view. Alexander ordered his tent to be pitched elsewhere on the river bank, the unit usually in attendance on him to stand guard before it, and all the sumptuous trappings of royalty to be deliberately flaunted before the enemy's eyes. Attalus, who was Alexander's age and not dissimilar to him in face and build (especially when seen at a distance), he also dressed in royal robes to make it appear that the king himself was protecting that part of the bank and not planning to cross.

The execution of this plan was first delayed, then assisted, by a storm, as fortune directed even disadvantages to a successful outcome. Alexander was preparing to cross the river with the rest of his troops in the direction of the island mentioned above, the enemy's attention having now been diverted to the men occupying the bank downstream with Ptolemy. At this point a storm let loose a downpour scarcely tolerable even under cover and, overwhelmed by the rainstorm, the soldiers fled back to shore, abandoning their boats and rafts. However, the roaring winds rendered the noise of their confusion inaudible to the enemy. Then, in an instant, the rain stopped, but the cloud cover was so thick that it blocked out the daylight and even men in conversation could barely make out each other's features. Another man would have been terrified by the darkness that shrouded the sky: they had to sail on a strange river, and the enemy was possibly occupying that very part of the bank to which they were directing their blind and reckless course. But the king derived glory from perilous situations, and he saw as his opportunity the darkness which frightened all the others. He gave the signal for all to board the rafts in silence and ordered the boat in which he himself was sailing to be pushed off first. The bank for which they were making was deserted by the enemy, for Porus' eyes were fixed entirely on Ptolemy. With the exception of one ship, stranded after a wave smashed it on to a rock, they all reached land and Alexander ordered his men to take up their arms and form ranks. (Curtius)

The battle progresses and, at one point, just as it seems Porus is defeated, he gains the advantage once again.

Porus, however, accompanied by a few whose sense of shame surpassed their fear, began to rally his scattered troops and to advance on his enemy, issuing instructions for the elephants to be driven before his line. The beasts caused great panic. Their strange trumpeting unsettled not only the horses – animals always very easily startled – but also the men in the ranks.

Victors moments before, the Macedonians were now casting around for a place to flee. Then Alexander sent the Agrianes and the Thracian light-armed against the elephants, for they were better at skirmishing than at fighting at close quarters. These released a thick barrage of missiles on both elephants and drivers, and the phalanx also proceeded to exert relentless pressure on the frightened animals. Some, however, pursued the elephants too energetically, provoking them to turn on them by the wounds they inflicted. Trampled underfoot, they served as a warning to the others to be more cautious in their pursuit. A particularly terrifying sight was when elephants would snatch up men in armour in their trunks and pass them over their heads to the drivers. So the fortunes of the battle kept shifting, with the Macedonians alternately chasing and fleeing from the elephants, and the contest dragged on inconclusively till late in the day. Then the Macedonians began to use axes – they had equipped themselves with such implements in advance – to hack off the elephants' feet, and they also chopped at the trunks of the animals with gently curving, sickle-like swords called *copides*. In their fear not just of dying, but of suffering novel kinds of torment as they died, they left nothing untried.

The elephants were finally exhausted by their wounds. They charged into their own men, mowing them down; their riders were flung to the ground and trampled to death. More terrified than menacing, the beasts were being driven like cattle from the battlefield when, mounted on his elephant, Porus, who had been deserted by most of his men, began to shower on the enemy swarming around him large numbers of javelins which he had set aside in advance. He wounded many Macedonians at long range but he was himself the target of weapons from every direction. He had already received nine wounds both to the back and to the chest, and had suffered severe loss of blood, so that the missiles he was throwing were slipping from his weakened hands rather than being hurled. His elephant, roused to a frenzy and as yet unwounded, attacked the enemy ranks no less aggressively than before, until its driver caught sight of his king in a barely conscious state, arms dangling and weapons fallen. At that he spurred the beast to flee. Alexander followed, but his horse was weak from taking many wounds and it toppled forward, setting the king on the ground rather than throwing him. Changing horses thus slowed down his pursuit.

In the meantime the brother of Taxiles, the Indian king, had been sent ahead by Alexander, and he began to advise Porus not to persevere to the end but to surrender to the victor. Although Porus' strength was spent and he had suffered considerable loss of blood, he started at the sound of this voice which he recognized. 'I know you,' he said, 'brother of Taxiles, traitor to his empire and his throne,' and he flung at him the one javelin which by chance had not fallen from his hands. It passed straight through his chest to emerge at the back. After this final courageous act, Porus began to flee with greater urgency, but his elephant had received numerous wounds and it also began to falter, so he stopped running and threw his infantry in the path of the pursuing enemy.

By now Alexander had caught up. He saw Porus' obstinacy and ordered that no mercy be shown to any who resisted. From every direction, missiles were showered on the Indian infantry and on Porus himself who, finally overwhelmed by them, began to slip from his elephant. The Indian driving it thought he was dismounting, and ordered the animal to come to its knees in the usual way. When the elephant crouched down the others also sank to the ground as they had been trained to do, and it was this that delivered Porus and the other Indians into the hands of the victors. Believing Porus dead, Alexander ordered his body to be stripped. Men quickly gathered to remove his cuirass and his clothing but then the elephant began protecting his master, attacking the men stripping him and lifting and setting Porus' body on his back once more. So the beast was subjected to a volley of weapons from every direction and, when he was dispatched, Porus was placed in a chariot.

Then Alexander saw him lift his eyes. Moved by pity, not hatred, he said to him, 'What folly forced you, knowing as you did the fame of my achievements, to try the fortunes of war, when Taxiles served as an example of my clemency towards those who surrender, an example so close to you?' 'Since you ask,' replied Porus, 'I shall answer you with the frankness your inquiry has granted me. I did not think there was anyone stronger than I. Though I knew my own strength, I had not yet tested yours, and now the outcome of the war has shown you to be the stronger. Even so, being second to you brings me no little satisfaction.'

Alexander questioned him further, asking his opinion on what his victor should do with him. 'What this day tells you to do,' said Porus, 'the day on which you have discovered how transitory good fortune is.' Porus' advice did him more good than pleas would have done. His greatness of spirit was not cowed or broken even in adversity, and Alexander felt obliged to treat him not only with mercy but with respect. He tended to his wounds just as if Porus had fought on his side and, when he recovered contrary to everyone's expectations, Alexander made him one of his friends and, shortly afterwards, bestowed on him an empire larger than he had formerly held. In fact, no trait of Alexander's was more firmly held or enduring than his admiration for genuine excellence and brilliant achievement, though he was fairer in his estimation of an enemy's praiseworthiness than a fellow citizen's, believing as he did that his own greatness could be eclipsed by his countrymen whereas it would be increased proportionately by the greatness of the peoples he defeated. (Curtius)

Alexander then founded two cities, one at the site of the battle, and the other at the spot where he had embarked on his crossing of the Hydaspes. The first was named Nicaea, in commemoration of his victory over the Indians; the second Bucephala, in memory of his horse Bucephalus, who had died here, not from any wound, but worn out by old age. He was about thirty years old and had succumbed to exhaustion, after enduring many hardships and dangers alongside Alexander. This Bucephalus was only ever mounted by Alexander, rejecting all other riders, and was a horse of great stature and noble spirit. According to some, he was branded with the shape of an ox-head, from which his name was said to originate. Yet others maintain that, though he was black, there was a white mark on his head, which bore a strong resemblance to the head of an ox. Having once lost him in Uxia, Alexander had proclaimed throughout the country that all the Uxians would be put to death unless they were to bring him back his horse. As soon as this proclamation was issued, the horse was returned: a testimony to both Alexander's devotion to his horse and the degree of fear he inspired among the natives. (Arrian)

Alexander was delighted to have won so memorable a victory which, he believed, opened up to him the limits of the East. He made a sacrifice of animals to the Sun and, to strengthen his men's enthusiasm for undertaking the remainder of the campaign, commended them publicly in a general assembly and declared that any strength the Indians had possessed had been shattered in the recent contest. From now on, he continued, they would have rich plunder: the area for which they were bound was renowned for its wealth. In fact, he said, the spoils from the Persians were cheap and paltry in comparison, and the soldiers would now fill Macedonia and Greece, not just their own homes, with pearls and precious stones, gold and ivory. The men were eager for both riches and glory and, since nothing Alexander had ever told them had proved to be wrong, they promised their support.

They were dismissed full of confidence, and Alexander ordered ships to be constructed so that after completing his expedition across Asia he might visit the sea at the world's end. Wood for ship-building was abundant on the neighbouring mountains. When they began cutting it, they came upon snakes of extraordinary size, and there were also rhinoceroses on the mountains, animals rare elsewhere. (Curtius)

Curtius mentions the snakes, but not the floods of the monsoon.

Abisares, who had sent a deputation to Alexander before the battle with Porus, now sent a second promising to allow all the king's commands on the one condition that he should not be forced to surrender himself, for he was prepared neither to live without royal power nor to rule as a prisoner. Alexander had word sent to him that, if he were reluctant to come to him, then Alexander would come to Abisares. After this he crossed the river and marched into the interior of India. Here almost interminable tracts of countryside were covered with forests darkened by tall trees that reached extraordinary heights. Most of the branches were like huge tree-trunks. They would bend down to the ground where they would turn and rise once more, creating the impression of being not a branch rising up again but a tree generated from an independent root.

The climate is healthy: the sun's intensity is alleviated by the shade and there are plentiful supplies of spring water. Here too, however, there were large numbers of snakes. They had scales which emitted a golden gleam and a venom of unique virulence – until the Macedonians were supplied with an antidote by the natives, a bite would be followed by instant death.

From here Alexander came through deserts to the river Hiarotis. Bordering the river was a well-shaded wood consisting of trees not found elsewhere and thickly populated by wild peacock. Moving camp from there, he took a nearby town with a military cordon and imposed tribute on it after taking hostages. He then proceeded to what was, for that region, a comparatively large city, which was protected by a marsh as well as a wall. The barbarians came forth to fight with chariots lashed together; some of them were equipped with spears, others with lances, and they would jump nimbly from chariot to chariot whenever they wished to aid comrades who were under pressure. At first this strange style of combat terrified the Macedonians, who were sustaining wounds at long range, but their fear was soon replaced by contempt for such undisciplined tactics and, surrounding the chariots on both sides, they began to cut down any offering resistance. Alexander ordered the lashings of the chariots to be severed so that the individual vehicles could be more easily surrounded, and the enemy, after losing 8,000 men, ran back into the town. The next day scaling ladders were put up on every side and the walls were taken. A few were saved by their speed: when they realized that the city was falling they swam across the marsh and struck sheer terror into the neighbouring towns with stories of the arrival of an invincible army, surely composed of gods!

Alexander now dispatched Perdiccas and a light-armed unit to ravage the area. He then transferred some of his troops to Eumenes so that he could help force the barbarians into submission, while Alexander himself led the remainder to a strongly fortified city in which the inhabitants of other cities had also sought refuge. The townspeople sent a delegation to intercede with the king but prepared for war all the same, for an argument had arisen which had split the people into two factions, some thinking any course preferable to surrender and others that they were unable to put up effective resistance. As they unsuccessfully tried to reach agreement, the party in favour of surrender flung open the gates and admitted the enemy. Although the war faction might have deserved his anger, Alexander nevertheless declared a general amnesty, accepted hostages and moved on to the next city. The hostages were taken along ahead of the troops and, when the inhabitants of the town recognized them as belonging to the same race as themselves, they invited them to parley. By emphasizing the king's mercy as well as his might, the hostages induced them to surrender, and the other cities were similarly subdued and given his assurance of protection.

From here the Macedonians came into the kingdom of Sophites. His nation, so barbarians believe, is pre-eminent in wisdom and governed by high moral principles. When children are born, whether they are acknowledged and how they are reared is decided not by the parents but by a group of people given the responsibility of examining the physical condition of infants. Those found to possess any abnormality or physical disability they order to be put to death. Marriage is based not on considerations of tribe or class but on physical attractiveness, since that is the criterion for judging children.

The town of this tribe to which Alexander had now advanced his troops was actually occupied by Sophites. The gates were closed but there were no armed men in evidence on the walls or parapets, and the Macedonians could not decide whether the inhabitants had abandoned the town or were lying in ambush. Suddenly a gate opened and the Indian king came out with his two adult sons. In handsomeness he far surpassed all other barbarians. His robe, which covered even his legs, was embroidered with gold and purple; his sandals were golden and studded with precious stones; his arms, both upper arm and forearm, were adorned with pearls; from his ears hung jewels of remarkable brilliance and size; his sceptre was of gold and decorated with beryl. The sceptre he now handed to Alexander with a prayer that good fortune should attend his taking it, and he surrendered himself together with his children and his people. (Curtius)

Alexander had received reports that on the other side of the Hyphasis lay a prosperous land, whose men were successful farmers, noble soldiers, and well-organized in the management of their internal affairs; although their governments were mainly aristocratic, the leadership was fair. The people also possessed far more elephants than the other Indians, magnificent beasts both in their size and their courage. Such reports only served to stir up Alexander's desire to advance, but Macedonian resolve was flagging, as the men watched their king pursuing a relentless campaign that was fraught with hardship and danger. Within the camp, meetings were taking place where the more moderate among them complained about their predicament, while others utterly refused to follow any further, even though Alexander was leading them. As soon as Alexander heard what was going on, and before the disorder and despondency among the soldiers could get any worse, he called a meeting of the commanders and gave the following speech:

'Now that I see that you, my Macedonians and allies, no longer have the spirit to follow me into dangers, I have called you together so that I might either persuade you and forge ahead, or let myself be persuaded to turn back. If, indeed, there is some cause for reproach regarding the hardship that you have endured up to now, or regarding my leadership, it is pointless for me to continue addressing you. Yet if, as the result of the hardship you have endured, you now occupy Ionia, the Hellespont, both Phrygias, Cappadocia, Paphlagonia, Lydia, Caria, Lycia, Pamphylia, Phoenicia and Egypt, together with the Greek part of Libya, much of Arabia, lowland Syria, Babylon and Susa; if you now rule over the peoples of Persia and Media and their former subjects, as well as those they did not rule; if you rule over the lands beyond the Caspian Gates, beyond the Caucasus, those beyond the Tanais, Bactria, Hyrcania and the Hyrcanian Sea; if we have driven back the Scythians into the desert; if, in addition to all this, even the river Indus runs through territory now ours, as do the Hydaspes, the Acesines and the Hydraotis, why then do you shrink from adding the Hyphasis and the peoples beyond the Hyphasis to your Macedonian empire? Are you afraid that those remaining natives will resist your approach? Not so. Some of them are actually willing to yield; those who flee are captured; others desert their country, enabling you to hand it over to those allies who joined us voluntarily.

'As far as I can see, true men need no reward for their labours aside from those labours themselves, as long as these have noble consequences. Nevertheless, if anyone should wish to know what limit is set for our campaign, let me tell him that it is only a small tract of land that now lies before us up to the river Ganges and the Eastern Ocean. I can tell you that you will find that this sea joins up with the Hyrcanian Sea; for the great Ocean flows around the whole of the earth. Moreover, I will prove to my Macedonians and allies that the Indian, Persian and Hyrcanian gulfs all flow together; and our fleet will sail from the Persian Gulf to Libya, as far as the Pillars of Hercules. Then all of Libya to the east shall be ours; indeed, all of Asia, so that the boundaries of this empire will be those that God has laid for the entire world.

'Should you turn back now, however, you will leave behind many warlike tribes on the other side of the Hyphasis as far as the Eastern Ocean, many more to the north and the Hyrcanian Sea, along with the Scythians who are also nearby. So, our retreat will pose the danger that those very nations that we now hold, but which are not secure, might be drawn into revolt by those over which we do not yet have control. Then, indeed, your many hardships will have been in vain; or you will need to begin again with fresh suffering and dangers. So, stand firm, men of Macedonia and our allies; for it is toil and danger that lead to glorious achievements, while pleasure lies in a life of courage and in a death that brings undying fame.' (Arrian)

In spite of Alexander's encouragement, the general Coenus replies that the men are weary and unwilling to proceed.

When Coenus finished speaking, his words were applauded. Some even shed tears, showing all the more their unwillingness to proceed with further dangers and the pleasure they would feel at retreating. Yet the freedom with which Coenus had spoken and the cowardice of the other officers angered Alexander, who now dismissed the assembly. On the following day he assembled them again, declaring that he himself would proceed, but would not force any of the Macedonians to accompany him against their will, since there would be men willing to follow their king. As for those who wished to return home, they were free to do so and to tell their people that they had returned, leaving their king in the midst of his enemies.

The speech concluded, he returned to his tent and for three days even his Companions were not allowed to enter. He was waiting to see whether the Macedonians and their allies would have a change of heart, as often happens among a group of soldiers, which would restore their obedience. Then, even though the camp remained utterly silent, and it was clear that far from changing the minds of his men his anger had in fact infuriated them, it is reported by Ptolemy, son of Lagus, that Alexander offered sacrifices for crossing the river. Yet the sacrificial victims turned out to be unfavourable and so, given that everything was now drawing him towards retreat, he finally called together the most senior and closest of his Companions and announced that he had now decided to turn back.

Some shouted with the cries of a rejoicing crowd, and many even began to weep. Then they approached Alexander's tent and called down great blessings upon him for allowing them to win over him, his sole defeat. Alexander then divided the army up into twelve sections and ordered a corresponding number of altars to be erected, their height equal to that of the greatest towers, their width even greater, as thank-offerings to the gods who had led him to so many victories, and as memorials of his labours. Once the altars were ready for him, he offered up the customary sacrifices upon them and held athletic contests for both his men and their horses. (Arrian)

8. THE RETREAT – FROM INDIA BACK TO PERSIA

Alexander returns to the Jhelum river and settles affairs in India, putting the kingdoms of the Punjab under the control of Porus. He sets off along the Indus and attacks the Malloi near the river Hydraotes. Having been severely wounded in the battle, he then returns downriver to his main army and sails off towards the ocean, arriving in July 325. From Pattala, Alexander sends the fleet westwards through the Persian Gulf and heads on by land. After the surrender of the rebellious Oreitae and Arabitae, he marches through southern Gedrosia, but the army suffers terribly from the severe heat and from lack of provisions. At the river Maxates he is reunited with the fleet and finds fresh provisions before advancing towards the capital of Gedrosia, Pura, with plans to march close to the coast of the Persian Gulf in order to support his fleet. However, on the sixty-day journey across the desert of Gedrosia (Makran), conditions are so harsh that thousands of his men perish. Meanwhile, in Alexander's absence, there have been revolts in over half of his provinces. Alexander suppresses rebellions in India and Persia and re-establishes his rule as he heads back into Persia in spring 324. At Susa, Alexander weds many of his troops to native noblewomen and takes two more brides himself. At this point he wishes to send home his veteran soldiers, whose age and weakness make them a liability. However, the veterans are unwilling to leave and resent Alexander's plan to replace them with the 30,000 young Persians who have been trained for the Macedonian army. At Opis, Alexander's plans to discharge his veterans are met by a minor mutiny which he swiftly dispels. The veterans finally give in and Alexander pacifies them with

*bonuses and other privileges. The army then heads north-east
to Ectabana. It is here that Hephaestion, Alexander's lover and
constant companion, dies, leaving Alexander distraught.*

Having given Porus command of the territory reaching all the
way to the river Hyphasis, he himself turned back towards the
Hydraotes. Once across the Hydraotes, he came back again
to the Acesines, where he found that the city that he had
ordered Hephaestion to fortify was already constructed. Here
he settled any of the local tribesmen who were willing, along
with those mercenaries who were unfit for service, while he
made preparations for his own voyage down to the Indian
Ocean. (Arrian)

Alexander was now eager to see the outer ocean. He had a large
number of oar-propelled ferries and rafts constructed, and was
rowed down the rivers on these at a leisurely speed. But his
voyage was by no means a peaceful and certainly not a passive
affair. As he travelled downstream he would land, assault the
cities near the banks, and subdue them all. However, when he
attacked the tribe known as the Malli, who are said to be the
most warlike of all the Indian peoples, he nearly lost his life.
After the defenders had been driven from the walls by volleys of
missiles, he was first to scramble to the top of the wall by means
of a scaling ladder. The ladder was smashed, so that no more
Macedonians could join him, and the barbarians began to gather
inside along the bottom of the wall and to shoot at him from
below. Finding himself almost alone and exposed to their
missiles, Alexander crouched down, leaped into their midst, and
by good luck landed on his feet. Then, as he brandished his
arms, it seemed to the barbarians as if a dazzling sheet of flame
suddenly took shape in front of his body, and they scattered and
fled. But when they saw that there were no more than two of
his Guards accompanying him, they rushed in to attack him.
Some of them engaged him hand to hand, and rained blows
upon his armour with sword and spear as he strove to defend
himself, while another, standing a little way apart, shot at him
with a bow. The shaft was so well aimed and struck him with

such force that it pierced his breastplate and lodged in his chest between the ribs. The impact was so violent that Alexander staggered back and sank to his knees; his attacker rushed up with his drawn scimitar in his hand, while Peucestas and Limmaeus threw themselves in front of him. Both men were wounded and Limmaeus was killed, but Peucestas stood firm, while Alexander killed the barbarian with his own hand. But he was wounded over and over again, and at last received a blow on the neck from a club which forced him to lean against the wall, although he still faced his assailants. At this moment the Macedonians swarmed round him, snatched him up as he lost consciousness, and carried him to his tent. Immediately the rumour ran through the camp that he had been killed. Meanwhile his attendants with great difficulty sawed off the wooden shaft of the arrow and thus succeeded in removing his breastplate; they then had to cut out the arrow-head, which was embedded between his ribs and measured, so we are told, four fingers' width in length and three in breadth. When it was extracted the king fainted away and came very near to death, but finally he recovered. Even when the danger was past he remained weak, and for a long time needed careful nursing and was obliged to remain on a diet. Then one day, as he heard a clamour outside his tent, he understood that the Macedonians were yearning to see him, and so he took his cloak and went out to them. After sacrificing to the gods, he once more boarded his vessel and proceeded down the river, subduing great cities and large tracts of territory as he went. (Plutarch)

After dealing with tribes such as the Arabitae and the Oreitae, Alexander and his men embark on a terrible march through southern Gedrosia.

From there he went on through Gedrosia along a difficult route, which yielded few supplies and, above all, rarely provided the army with water. Moreover, they were forced to march through much of the territory by night and a long way from the sea, although Alexander was very keen to proceed along the country's coastline in order to see what harbours there were and, if possible, to help the fleet either by digging wells or by setting up trading posts and anchorages. (Arrian)

Alexander gathers provisions and sets off across the desert of Gedrosia.

Alexander then headed for the capital of Gedrosia, in the district known as Pura, arriving there sixty days after leaving Oria. Many writers report that the great hardship that his army endured in Asia cannot be compared to the suffering they endured on this journey. It was not due to ignorance of the route's difficulties that Alexander opted to go this way (Nearchus is the only one to mention this), but because he had heard that, apart from Semiramis on her retreat from India, no one had managed to bring their army through along this route. According to native reports, even Semiramis had survived with only twenty of her soldiers, while Cyrus, son of Cambyses, made it with just seven. In fact, Cyrus had come to this region in order to invade India, but, before he could achieve his aim, most of his army had perished during the deserted and barren journey. Such stories inspired Alexander to try and outdo Cyrus and Semiramis; and this, together with his desire to provide the nearby fleet with provisions, is the reason why he chose this route, according to Nearchus.

Now the blistering heat and lack of water destroyed much of the army, especially the pack animals, most of which died of thirst or were overwhelmed by the depth and heat of the sand, as they came across high hills of deep and loose sand, into which they would sink as if they were walking in mud or even untrodden snow. The horses and mules suffered even more from the uneven and unsafe tracks on which they ascended and descended. For the soldiers, the unpredictable lengths of the marches were a terrible ordeal, as no one knew where water would next be found. Whenever the men, having covered the necessary distance during the night, found water at dawn, their distress was not so great; but when they found themselves still marching well into the day, they suffered terribly from the effects of exhaustion combined with incessant thirst.

Although among the pack animals the losses were heavy, it was often the army themselves who were responsible for their deaths. Whenever they ran out of provisions, the men would get together and slaughter large numbers of horses and mules to eat their flesh, claiming that these animals had died of thirst or collapsed from exhaustion; and no one would point out the full truth of this crime because they had all been joint perpetrators, overwhelmed by their suffering. In fact, although Alexander was aware of these events, he decided that the men's current predicament would be better served if he was to feign ignorance rather than admit that he knew what was going on. To make matters worse, soon the transportation of the sick and those who had collapsed from exhaustion along the way became difficult: not only was there a lack of pack animals, but the men had been deliberately destroying the wagons, which could not be dragged along through the deep sand and had, in the early stages, led to them taking the routes which were easiest for the animals, rather than those which were shortest. And so it happened that some were abandoned along the way, either sick or simply no longer able to withstand the exhaustion, the heat or the thirst. They could neither be carried, nor looked after, for the men's overriding desire to press on with the march as speedily as they could meant that they had to forget any concern for individuals. Some of them were actually overwhelmed by sleep during the marches, since these usually took place during the night. Only a few, those who woke up and still had the strength to follow the army's tracks, survived, but most of them perished, sinking into the sand as though it were the sea.

Yet there were still further misfortunes in store for the army, which brought the very worst suffering to the men and to their horses and pack animals. Just as in India, the monsoon winds bring heavy rains to Gedrosia, which fall not on the Gedrosian plains but in the mountains, where the clouds are carried by the winds and, unable to clear the crests, release their rains. The army had stopped for the night by a small stream, for the sake of its water. Around the second watch of the night, the stream was suddenly swollen by the rains, which had fallen out of sight of the army, and its waters spread out to them with such force that most of the women and children of those who followed the camp were drowned, while the whole royal compound was swept away, together with all the remaining pack animals; the men themselves barely escaped, carrying only their weapons, and not even all of these.

To add to their ordeal, whenever suffering from heat and thirst, they found a plentiful supply of water, many died as a consequence of unrestrained drinking. Accordingly, Alexander tended to set up camp about a couple of miles away from the water, rather than right at its edge, so that the men would not destroy themselves and their animals by rushing at it in a frenzy, and so that the most desperate among them would not ruin the water for the rest of the army by jumping into the spring or the stream.

At this point, I think it would be wrong to leave one of Alexander's most noble achievements unrecorded, regardless of whether it took place here or, earlier, among the Parapamisadae, as others have written. In their need to reach water the army was marching through the sand, the heat already scorching, and there was some way to go. Alexander, who was himself suffering from thirst, still managed to lead the way on foot in spite of the difficulties, hoping that, as often happens at such times, the fact that he was sharing their misfortune would make it easier for his troops to bear. Meanwhile some of the light infantry, who had gone ahead from the other soldiers to search for water, came across a paltry pool of water which had collected in some shallow gully. They filled a pouch with it and rushed back to Alexander, as if they bore some fantastic prize. Once they had approached they handed over the water, poured into a helmet, to their king. Alexander then took the water and, praising those who had brought it, poured it away in full view of all his men, an action which gave the army such strength that it seemed as though every man had actually drunk the water that Alexander had thrown away. In my opinion it is for this action, above all others, that we should praise Alexander's leadership and endurance.

There were still further problems, when the guides finally admitted that they could no longer remember the way, now that the direction markers had vanished, blown away by the wind; for the vast piles of sand around them were all alike and provided no indication of the route: there were no trees growing along the road, nor were there any hills that might not have shifted. Moreover, the guides were not even skilled in navigating by the stars at night or by the sun during the day; they could not, as Phoenician sailors do, use the Little Bear to orient themselves, nor could they, as others do, use the Great Bear. At this juncture, Alexander decided that the way lay to the left and went on ahead with a few of the horsemen; when the horses became exhausted from the heat, he left most of them behind and rode on with just five. Finally they found the sea and scraped away the pebbles on the beach to reveal pure fresh water. Now the whole army followed and, for seven days, they marched along the coast, drawing water from the beach, until the route once again became familiar to the guides and they were able to head back inland.

When they arrived at the capital of Gedrosia, the troops rested. Alexander appointed Thoas to the satrapy after removing Apollophanes, when he realized that Apollophanes had failed to carry out any of his orders. (Arrian)

Alexander himself went on to Susa, where he arrested and executed Abulites, along with his son Oxathres, because he had acted improperly while managing affairs there. Among the rulers of those countries captured by Alexander, there had been considerable abuses perpetrated against temples, tombs, and even the subjects themselves; for the king's Indian expedition had gone on for a long time and it was widely believed that he would not return from his encounters with so many tribes and elephants, but would perish somewhere beyond the Indus, Hydaspes, Acesines and Hyphasis. The recent disasters he had experienced in Gedrosia, had further encouraged the satraps to reject the idea of his homecoming altogether. At the same time, Alexander himself is at this point reported to have become more swiftly persuaded by accusations of wrongdoing, believing them to be entirely reliable, and to have taken extreme measures against those who were convicted of even small misdemeanours, because he felt that the attitude of such men might lead them on to greater crimes.

At Susa he also organized weddings for himself and his Companions. He took Barsine, Darius' eldest daughter, as his wife and, according to Aristobulus, another wife, Parysatis, the youngest daughter of Ochus, although he was already married to Roxane, the daughter of Oxyartes the Bactrian. He gave another of Darius' daughters – Drypetis, his own wife's sister – to Hephaestion because he wanted to be the uncle of Hephaestion's children. He gave Amastrine, daughter of Darius' brother Oxathres, to Craterus; a daughter of Atropates, the satrap of Media, to Perdiccas; the daughters of Artabazus, Artacama and Artonis, to his bodyguard Ptolemy and his secretary Eumenes respectively; the daughter of Barsine and Mentor to Nearchus; and the daughter of the Bactrian Spitamenes to Seleucus. In this way, about eighty of the most important Persian and Median daughters became the wives of Companions, and the weddings were celebrated according to Persian custom. Thrones were set up for the bridegrooms in order of importance and, once toasts had been made, the brides came in and sat by the sides of their grooms, who then took them by the hand and kissed them. All the weddings took place together, the king marrying first and showing, more than ever, that in his actions he was a man of the people and did not put himself above his friends. Once the grooms had received their brides, they took them to their homes, each of them provided with a dowry by Alexander. As for the other Macedonians who also married Asian women, more than 10,000 of them, Alexander ordered that a list of their names should be drawn, so that they would all receive wedding gifts from him. (Arrian)

The 30,000 boys whom he had left behind to be given a Greek education and military training had now grown into active and handsome men and had developed a wonderful skill and agility in their military exercises. Alexander was delighted with their progress, but the Macedonians were disheartened and deeply disturbed for their own future, because they assumed that the king would henceforth have less regard for them. So when he arranged to send the sick and disabled among them to the sea coast, they protested that he was not only doing them an injustice but deliberately humiliating them. He had first worn them out in every kind of service, and now he was turning them away in disgrace and throwing them upon the mercy of their parents and native cities, where they would be in worse care than when they had set out for Asia. Why not send them all home and write off the Macedonians as useless, now that he had this corps of young ballet-soldiers, with whom he could go on to conquer the world? These words stung Alexander and he angrily rebuked the Macedonians, dismissed his Guards, handed over their security duties to Persians and recruited from these his royal escort and personal attendants. When the Macedonians saw him surrounded by these men, while they were barred from his presence and treated as being in disgrace, they were greatly humbled, and when they considered the matter, they understood that they had been almost beside themselves with jealousy and rage. Finally, when they had come to their senses, they presented themselves at Alexander's tent unarmed and dressed only in their tunics, and there they cried out and lamented, threw themselves on his mercy and begged him to deal with them as their baseness and ingratitude deserved. Alexander refused to receive them, although he had already begun to relent, but the men would not go away and remained for two days and nights outside his tent weeping and calling him their master. At last on the third day he came out, and when he saw them reduced to such a forlorn and pitiful state, he himself wept for a while. He reproached them gently for their behaviour and finally spoke to them kindly: afterwards he dismissed those who were no longer fit for service and gave them generous gratuities. Besides this he sent instructions to Antipater that at all public contests and in the theatres these men should occupy the best seats and wear garlands on their heads. He also gave orders that the orphaned children of those who had died in his service should continue to receive their fathers' pay. (Plutarch)

At this time it happened that Hephaestion had caught a fever, and, being a young man who was accustomed to a soldier's life, he could not bear to remain on a strict diet. No sooner had his physician Glaucus gone off to the theatre than he sat down to breakfast, devoured a boiled fowl and washed it down with a great coolerful of wine. His fever quickly mounted and soon afterwards he died. Alexander's grief was uncontrollable. As a sign of mourning he gave orders that the manes and tails of all horses should be shorn, demolished the battlements of all the neighbouring cities, crucified the unlucky physician and forebade the playing of flutes or any other kind of music for a long time until finally an oracle was announced from the temple of Ammon, commanding him to honour Hephaestion and sacrifice to him as a hero. To lighten his sorrow he set off on a campaign, as if the tracking down and hunting of men might console him, and he subdued the tribe of the Cossaeans, massacring the whole male population from the youths upwards: this was termed a sacrifice to the spirit of Hephaestion. He determined to spend 10,000 talents on the funeral and the tomb for his friend, and as he wished the ingenuity and originality of the design to surpass the expense he was especially anxious to employ Stasicrates, as this artist was famous for his innovations, which combined an exceptional degree of magnificence, audacity and ostentation. (Plutarch)

9. ALEXANDER'S
FINAL MONTHS

In winter 324 Alexander leaves Ectabana and goes to Babylon, where he is plagued by a series of bad omens. Frightened, but undeterred, he prepares for an expedition against the Arabs by strengthening his fleet and planning towns and harbours on the banks of the Euphrates. A mid-June departure is settled for the Arabian expedition, but Alexander is never to leave Babylon. On 29 May 323 he attends a party given by one of his Companions, Medius, after which he is taken ill. He dies some two weeks later, on 10 June. Reports of his death are varied and the cause is uncertain, with some claiming that he died from over-drinking, some from illness, and others that he was poisoned.

Towards the end of the year Alexander travelled to Babylon. Before he arrived he was joined by Nearchus, who had sailed through the ocean and up the Euphrates: Nearchus told him that he had met some Chaldaeans who had advised the king to stay away from Babylon. Alexander paid no attention to this warning and continued his journey, but then he arrived before the walls of the city, he saw a large number of ravens flying about and pecking one another, and some of them fell dead in front of him. Next he received a report that Apollodorus, the governor of Babylon, had offered up a sacrifice to try to discover what fate held in store for Alexander, and he then sent for Pythagoras, the diviner who had conducted the sacrifice. Pythagoras admitted that this was true, and Alexander then asked him in what condition he had found the victim. 'The liver,' Pythagoras told him, 'had no lobe.' 'Indeed,' replied Alexander, 'that is a threatening omen.' He did Pythagoras no harm and he began to regret that he had not taken Nearchus' advice, and so he spent most of his time outside the walls of Babylon, either in his tent or in boats on the Euphrates. Many more omens now occurred to trouble him. A tame ass attacked the finest lion in his menagerie and kicked it to death. On another occasion Alexander took off his clothes for exercise and played a game of ball. When it was time to dress again, the young men who had joined him in the game suddenly noticed that there was a man sitting silently on the throne and wearing Alexander's diadem and royal robes. When he was questioned, he could say nothing for a long while, but later he came to his senses and explained that he was a citizen of Messenia named Dionysius. He had been accused of some crime, brought to Babylon from the coast, and kept for a long time in chains. Then the god Serapis had appeared to him, cast off his chains and brought him to this place, where he had commanded him to put on the king's robe and diadem, take his seat on the throne and hold his peace.

When he had heard the man's story, Alexander had him put to death, as the diviners recommended. But his confidence now deserted him, he began to believe that he had lost the favour of the gods, and he became increasingly suspicious of his friends. It was Antipater and his sons whom he feared most of all. One of them, named Iollas, was his chief cup-bearer. The other, Cassander, had only lately arrived in Babylon, and when he saw some of the barbarians prostrate themselves before the king, he burst into loud and disrespectful laughter, for he had been brought up as a Greek and had never seen such a spectacle in his life. Alexander was furious at this insult, seized him by the hair with both hands and dashed his head against the wall. On another occasion when Cassander wished to reply to some men who were making accusations against his father Antipater, Alexander interrupted him and said, 'What do you mean? Are you really saying that these men have suffered no wrong, but have travelled all this way just to bring a false accusation?' When Cassander replied that the very fact of their having travelled so far from those who could contradict them might point to the charges being false, Alexander laughed and said, 'This reminds

me of some of Aristotle's sophisms, which can be used equally
well on either side of a question: but if any of you are proved to
have done these men even the smallest wrong, you will be sorry
for it.' In general, we are told, this fear was implanted so deeply
and took such hold of Cassander's mind that even many years
later, when he had become king of Macedonia and master of
Greece, and was walking about one day looking at the sculptures
at Delphi, the mere sight of a statue of Alexander struck him with
horror, so that he shuddered and trembled in every limb, his head
swam and he could scarcely regain control of himself. (Plutarch)

While the triremes were being built and the harbour was being
dug in Babylon, Alexander sailed from Babylon down the Euphrates to the river known as Pallacopas, which is found about
100 miles downriver from Babylon and is itself a canal flowing
from the Euphrates, rather than a river rising from its own
springs. On its course from the Armenian hills during the winter,
the Euphrates is not deep and flows within its banks, whereas
when spring arrives, and especially around the summer solstice,
it becomes a great river and bursts its banks into the Armenian
countryside. This happens because during this season the melting snow from the Armenian mountains swells the river a great
deal, raising its water level, so that it overflows on to the land –
or at least it used to. Now this flooding is prevented by an
opening that takes the excess water down the Pallacopas into
the marshes and lakes which stretch without a break from this
canal right up to Arabia; from there it flows primarily through
the swamps, from which it runs out into the sea through a
number of indistinct channels. Then, once the snow has melted,
around the setting of the Pleiades, the Euphrates subsides,
although it still discharges much of its water down the Pallacopas into the lakes. In fact, if the Pallacopas was not blocked
off by a sluice at one point, the entire Euphrates would drain
into the canal and would not supply water to the Assyrian
plains. The Euphrates' outlet into the Pallacopas was therefore
closed off, at great effort, by the satrap of Babylon; yet it
nevertheless easily opened up again because the land there is
muddy and mainly consists of the type of clay that lets in river

water; it was thus difficult to turn the river back, even though more than 10,000 Assyrians were working on the project continuously for three months.

When Alexander learnt about the situation, he felt compelled to help Assyria and decided to close up securely the outlet through which the Euphrates flows into the Pallacopas. He found, however, that the ground about four miles from there was stony and, if quarried so that there was an opening from that point into the existing Pallacopas canal, the solidity of the earth would prevent the water from seeping out, and a sluice would easily contain it during the rainy season. With such aim in mind, Alexander sailed to the Pallacopas and travelled down the canal to the lakes, in the direction of Arabia. Here he found a good site and constructed and fortified a new town, where he settled any of the Greek mercenaries who volunteered and any of his men rendered unfit for service either by old age or by injury.

Alexander now felt as if he had proved the Chaldaean prophecy to be untrue, since he had marched out of Babylon without suffering any of the harm that they had foretold, and he sailed off again through the marshlands in good spirits, keeping Babylon to his left. Nevertheless, part of the fleet which was without a guide got lost among the narrow channels, until Alexander sent someone who would be able to bring them back on course.

There is a tale to tell about the events which took place at this point. Most of the tombs of the Assyrian kings are built in these lakes and marshes and, while Alexander was sailing through the marshes, steering the trireme himself (as the story goes), a strong gust of wind struck his sun-hat and the royal diadem that was attached to it. Now the hat was heavy and fell into the water, but the diadem was carried off and got caught up on one of the reeds that had grown next to an ancient royal tomb. This in itself could be taken as a sign of what was to come, but then the following also occurred: one of the sailors swam off to retrieve the diadem from the reed; unable to carry it in his hands, since it would have got wet as he swam, he wrapped it around his own head. Many historians report that Alexander rewarded him with a talent for his enthusiasm, but then gave orders for him to be beheaded, because the seers had advised him that he should not allow the head that had worn the royal diadem to remain alive. Aristobulus claims, however, that the talent was given to the sailor, and that he was only whipped for having worn the diadem. Some say that this sailor was Seleucus, and that this event was a portent of Alexander's death and Seleucus' mighty empire; for it is indisputable that Seleucus was the greatest king to succeed Alexander, having the most royal mind, but also, with the exception of Alexander, ruling over the greatest territory.

On his return to Babylon, Alexander found that Peucestas has come from Persia with an army of 20,000 Persians, including many Cossaean and Tapurian soldiers as these were reputed to be the best fighters among Persia's neighbouring tribes. He was joined too by Philoxenus, leading an army from Caria; Menander, bringing more soldiers from Lydia; and Menidas, with the cavalry that had been put under his command. Meanwhile embassies were also arriving from Greece, their envoys donning ceremonial garlands and approaching Alexander to lay golden crowns upon him, as if they had in fact come to pay reverence to a god. Yet, in spite of all this, Alexander's end was drawing near. (Arrian)

A few days later Alexander was feasting and drinking late into the night with his friends after offering the usual sacrifices to the gods for good fortune, as well as performing other rites that the seers had advised. It is also said that he had given out sacrificial victims and wine to each of the sections and units of the army. Some report that he actually wanted to leave the celebrations and retire to bed, but that he was met by Medius, the most trusted of his Companions at that time, who asked him to join him for more drinking, promising a good party. The royal Diaries state that he did carry on drinking with Medius, and then left to bathe and sleep before rejoining Medius again to feast and drink late into the night. Having left the drinking once more, he bathed and fell asleep immediately, already succumbing to a fever.

Every day he was brought out on his bed to perform the customary rites and then lay in the men's quarters until dusk. Meanwhile he gave the officers instructions that those who were to continue by foot should be ready to start marching in three days time, while those who were to sail with him would set sail in four. From the men's quarters, he was taken to the river on his bed and boarded a boat to cross over to the other side, to a park where he bathed again and rested. The next day he bathed once more and performed his sacrifices, then entered his room to lie down and chat to Medius, ordering his officers to come to him at dawn. After a light meal he was taken back to his room, where he lay in a fever throughout the night, then rose the following day to bathe and perform the sacrifices. He gave instructions to Nearchus and the other commanders regarding their journey as they were due to set sail in two days' time; but the following day, once he had bathed and carried out the necessary sacrifices, he found no relief from the fever. Nevertheless, he summoned his officers to tell them to ensure that everything would be ready for the voyage; but, after bathing in the evening, he became seriously ill. The next day he was taken to the house near the baths and made his sacrifices, before calling on his chief officers again, in spite of his sickness to give instructions about the voyage. While it was barely possible to take him to perform the sacrificial rites the following day, he was still issuing his commanders with orders for the journey. But, on the day after that, though his illness did not prevent him from performing his sacrifices, he gave orders for his generals to wait in the court, and for the other commanders to stand in front of his door. His condition had now utterly deteriorated and when he was brought to the palace from the park he recognized his officers as they came in, but no longer addressed them, remaining silent. Through the next two nights and days he lay in a high fever.

These events are all recorded in the royal Diaries. They go on to report that Alexander's men were desperate to see him; some, so that they could catch a glimpse of him while he was still alive; while others had heard that he was already dead and were suspicious, I think that his bodyguards were keeping his death a secret; most were driven by grief and longing for their king to force their way in to see him. It is said that he had already lost the power of speech when his men filed past, but greeted each of them by raising his head slightly and acknowledging them with a glance. The Diaries also relate how Peithon, Attalus, Demophon and Peucestas, as well as Cleomenes, Menidas and Seleucus all stayed the night in the temple of Serapis, asking the god whether Alexander would be better off being brought into the temple and praying for recovery. However, a pronouncement came from the god to say that Alexander should not be brought into the temple, but would be better served by remaining where he was. Shortly after the Companions made known these divine words, Alexander passed away – for this was now the 'better' thing.

Although there is no record of subsequent events in either Aristobulus or Ptolemy, others have written that when his Companions asked him to whom he was leaving his kingdom, he replied 'to the best'. Some also say that he added the further remark that he could see that great funeral games would be held in his honour.

I know that there have also been many other tales told about Alexander's death. One such story is that he died after being poisoned by a drug sent to him by Antipater; Aristotle is said to have made up this poison because Callisthenes' death had made him fear Alexander, and Cassander, son of Antipater, to have brought it to Alexander. Others even say that he brought it in the hoof of a mule, and that Iollas Cassander's younger brother, gave it to Alexander; for Iollas was the royal cup-bearer and had been offended in some way by Alexander shortly before his death. According to other reports, Medius was in love with Iollas and played some part in this affair – it was, after all, Medius who had invited Alexander to the party, and Alexander had retired from the drinking after experiencing a sharp pain when he drained his cup. A certain writer has even gone so far as to claim that when Alexander realized he was going to die, he went to throw himself into the river Euphrates, so that his disappearance would make it more plausible for posterity to believe that he had been born from a god and had now returned to the gods. However, his wife Roxane saw that he was about to leave and held him back, at which he cried out at her that she begrudged him the immortal frame of having been born from a god. I have told these stories so as to prove that I am not ignorant of them, not because these tales are in any way credible.

Alexander died in the 114th Olympiad, while Hegesias was archon at Athens. Aristobulus says that he lived for thirty-two years and eight months, and that he ruled for twelve years and these final eight months. He was handsome, embraced hardship and had the sharpest of minds; he was extremely brave and dedicated himself both to honour and to taking risks, while also showing great devotion to the gods. With bodily pleasures he was most restrained; as far as those of the mind were concerned, he had an insatiable appetite for glory alone. Even when circumstances were unclear, he was highly skilled in seeing what needed to be done, and he had great success in his understanding of those things which could be observed. When it came to drawing up, arming and equipping his army, he was highly knowledgeable; yet he was also most noble on any occasion when he was to raise morale among the soldiers, to fill them with hopes, and, through his own fearlessness, to dispel their fear in times of danger. At moments of uncertainty, he acted with the greatest courage; he showed the greatest skill in anticipating and outstripping the enemy, before they even had time to fear what would happen. He kept to his promises and agreements most firmly, but also showed great care not to fall prey to deception. Highly reluctant to spend money for his own pleasure, he gave liberally for the benefit of others.

It is true that passion or temper may have sometimes led Alexander astray, that to some degree he inclined towards the arrogance of eastern potentates; but, in my opinion, this is of no great consequence, as long as one makes some allowance for Alexander's youth, for his unceasing success, and for those people who seek out royal company offering flattery rather than genuine assistance, and whose association will always be of harm. Moreover, Alexander alone of the kings of old was noble enough to repent for his errors; whereas most people, even when they recognize that they are in the wrong, are led by their bad judgement to suppose that they can hide their error by defending it, as if they had in fact acted correctly. I believe, however, that the only cure for wrongdoing is to admit one's guilt and show one's repentance, as the sufferings of those who have been wronged will be alleviated if the wrongdoer acknowledges his crimes; while he himself may have some hope of avoiding future errors, if he is distressed by those he has already committed.

Once again, I do not consider that Alexander committed some grave offence by claiming divine origin; most likely, it was just some device to elevate his stature among his subjects. In fact, to me he seems no less illustrious a king than Minos, Aeacus or Rhadamanthus, all of whom attributed their parentage to Zeus without being seen as hubristic by the men of old; and the same is true of Theseus with Poseidon and Ion with Apollo. I also feel that his adoption of Persian dress was intended to show the Persians that the king was not wholly foreign and to indicate to the Macedonians some shift away from sharp Macedonian arrogance, while similar reasons seem to have been behind his decision to introduce Persian soldiers, the 'bearers of the golden apples', among the Macedonians, and Persian nobility into the divisions. Even his drinking bouts, as Aristobulus explains, were not drawn out because of his greed for wine – for Alexander was not a heavy drinker – but because he loved to spend time with his friends.

Whoever would reproach Alexander, let him do this not only on the basis of any of his actions which are worthy of reproach, but after taking into account all of his actions; moreover, let him first weigh up his own personality and achievements against who Alexander was and the extent of his mortal prosperity, as he became the indisputable king of both continents and achieved universal renown; by comparison, the man who offers such reproaches will then recognize his own lack of consequence and his failure to bring even his pathetic labours to fruition.

It is my opinion that, at that time, there was no nation, no city, not even one man, who had not heard the name of Alexander. To my mind, it does then seem implausible, that this man should bear no trace of divinity. This seems to be borne out by some of the oracles which predicted his death; by the various visions and dreams experienced by numbers of people; and by the immortal esteem and remembrance in which he is still held among human-kind; even now, after such a length of time, there are still further oracles that testify to the glory of both Alexander and the Macedonian people. (Arrian)

Sources

The texts selected in our book are taken from the following sources: Arrian: *The Campaigns of Alexander*, Curtius: *The History of Alexander* and Plutarch: *Alexander*. The sources are given below in the order in which the excerpts appear.

1. THE EARLY YEARS

Plutarch 2–10.

2. ESTABLISHING POWER IN MACEDONIA, GREECE AND NORTHERN EUROPE

Plutarch 11; Arrian 1; Plutarch 14.

3. THE PERSIAN CAMPAIGN (1) – FROM THE HELLESPONT TO GORDIUM

Plutarch 15–16; Arrian 1.16; Plutarch 17; Arrian 1.18; Plutarch 17–18.

4. THE PERSIAN CAMPAIGN (2) – FROM CAPPADOCIA TO EGYPT

Arrian 2.1; Curtius 3.2; Arrian 2.4; Plutarch 20–21; Plutarch 24; Curtius 4.2.2–4.4.18; Arrian 2.26; Curtius 4.7–4.8.3.

5. THE PERSIAN CAMPAIGN (3) – VICTORY
IN PERSIA

Plutarch 31–2; Curtius 4.15–4.16.9; Arrian 3.16; Plutarch 37–8;
Arrian 3.21–3.22; Plutarch 44–5.

6. TO THE NORTH-EAST FRONTIERS OF THE
PERSIAN EMPIRE

Arrian 3.25; Curtius 7.3–7.4.7; Curtius 7.4.20–7.4.25; Curtius 7.5.1–
7.6.9; Arrian 4.1–2; Arrian 4–7; Arrian 4.8; Arrian 4.16; Arrian 4.18;
Plutarch 54; Curtius 8.6; Curtius 8.20–23.

7. EAST INTO INDIA – THE UNCOMPLETED
CAMPAIGN

Curtius 8.10.1–9; Arrian 4.28–4.30; Arrian 5.8; Curtius 8.13.6–
8.13.27; Curtius 8.14.22–8.14.46; Arrian 5.19; Curtius 9.1.1–5; Curtius 9.1.7–9.1.29; Arrian 5.25–5.26; Arrian 5.28–5.29.

8. THE RETREAT – FROM INDIA BACK
TO PERSIA

Arrian 5.29; Plutarch 63; Arrian 6.23; Arrian 6.24; Arrian 7.4–7.5;
Plutarch 71–2.

9. ALEXANDER'S FINAL MONTHS

Plutarch 73–4; Arrian 7.21–7.23; Arrian 7.24–7.30.

Glossary of Main Characters

Abisares Indian ruler of the Kashmir area.

Abulites Satrap of Susiana under Darius III, he surrendered Susa to Alexander in late 331.

Amyntas Son of Adromenes. He commanded a battalion of the Macedonian phalanx at Issus.

Antipater Regent of Macedon from 334 until his death in 319 BC. Rumour held that he poisoned Alexander.

Aretes Commander of the lancers (*sarisophori*), he was sent against the Scythians who were plundering the Macedonian baggage at the battle of Arbela (Gaugamela).

Aristander Alexander's seer from Telmessus.

Aristotle The famous Athenian philosopher, who tutored Alexander in his youth.

Arsaces Governor of Aria, who succeeded Satibarzanes.

Artabazus A faithful courtier of Darius who later submitted to Alexander and was made satrap of Bactria.

Attalus Commander of the Agrianes.

Bagistanes A Babylonian, he brought Alexander news of Darius' impending arrest.

Barsaentes Satrap of the Drangae, he was one of the murderers of Darius.

Barsine Daughter of Artabazus and wife of Memnon, she was captured by Parmenion at Damascus. She became intimate with Alexander.

Bessus Darius' satrap of Bactria, he joined the king before the battle of Gaugamela, but his loyalty was suspect.

Calas Probably a cousin of Harpalus the treasurer, he ruled Hellespontine Phrygia.

Callisthenes Alexander's official historian, the nephew of Aristotle.

Catanes A follower of Bessus; together with Spitamenes and Dataphernes, he arrested Bessus and delivered him to Alexander.

Charidemus Exiled from Athens on Alexander's order, he joined Darius.

Cleander Son of Polemocrates and, apparently, the brother of Coenus.

Cleitus Commander of the 'Royal Squadron' of Alexander's cavalry. Alexander killed him after a drunken quarrel at Maracanda in 327 BC. Also known as 'Black' Cleitus.

Coenus Son of Polemocrates and, apparently, the brother of Cleander. At the Hyphasis he was the spokesman of the soldiers and urged Alexander to turn back.

Craterus One of Alexander's leading generals.

Darius Darius III 'Codamannus', King of Persia 336–330 BC.

Dataphernes A Bactrian noble. Together with Catanes and Spitamenes, he arrested Bessus to hand him over to Alexander.

Epimenes One of the pages who conspired with Hermolaus to kill Alexander.

Eurylochus Brother of Epimenes, who had been a fellow conspirator with Hermolaus.

Harpalus Alexander's treasurer and personal friend.

Hephaestion Alexander's dearest friend and lover, but a man of questionable military ability.

Hermolaus Son of Sopolis; a page. He was punished by Alexander for killing a boar which the king intended to strike. Hermolaus then conspired with Sostratus and a number of other pages to murder the king.

Lysimachus Alexander's tutor, bodyguard and kinsman.

Mazaces Ruler of Egypt. In 332 he surrendered Memphis and its treasures to Alexander.

Mazaeus A prominent Persian commander.

Meleager A Macedonian phalanx commander.

Memnon Rhodian mercenary leader; husband of Barsine and son-in-law of Artabazus. His death changed the complexion of the war in Asia Minor and brought Darius into direct conflict with Alexander.

Menes a prominent Macedonian and bodyguard of Alexander. He was ordered to guard the treasure Alexander sent home for the retired Thessalian cavalry.

Menidas Commander of the mercenary cavalry at Gaugamela.

Nabarzanes Darius' *chiliarchos* (captain). With Bessus, he plotted to arrest and murder Darius.

Nearchus Alexander's personal friend and fleet commander.

Nicanor Son of Parmenion and commander of the hypaspists. He died shortly before the Philotas affair in 330.

Olympias Married Philip II in 357 BC. Mother of Alexander.

Orontobates Together with Ariobarzanes he commanded the Persians, Mardians and Sogdiani at Gaugamela.

Oxathres Brother of Darius III.

Oxyartes A Sogdian baron.

Parmenion Alexander's foremost general until 330 BC. Father of Philotas, Hector and Nicanor.

Pausanias Assassin of Philip II.

Perdiccas A prominent commander and trusted friend of Alexander, Perdiccas was the most powerful individual in Babylon at the time of Alexander's death.

Peucestas Saved Alexander's life in India in 325.

Philotas Son of Parmenion and commander of the Companion cavalry. Implicated in a conspiracy against Alexander and executed.

Polemon Son of Adromenes. Brother of Amyntas.

Porus One of the most powerful of the Indian kings, who ruled the lands between the Hydaspes and Acesines rivers and opposed Alexander at the Hydaspes. He later entered into a friendly alliance with him and retained his kingdom.

Ptolemy Macedonian officer and friend of Alexander; king of Egypt 305–283 BC.

Roxane Daughter of Oxyartes, she married Alexander.

Satibarzanes Satrap of Aria.

Sitalces One of Parmenion's murderers.

Sophites Indian king who ruled territory between the Hydraotes and the Hyphasis.

Sostratus Son of Amyntas. A page and lover of Hermolaus, he conspired against Alexander.

Spitamenes Bactrian noble who, together with Dataphernes and Catanes, arrested Bessus.

Taxiles Formerly known as Omphis, with Alexander's consent he became ruler of Taxila and took the name Taxiles.

Thais An Athenian courtesan, later the mistress of Ptolemy, she induced Alexander to burn the palace at Persepolis.

Xerxes King of Persia (485–465 BC who invaded Greece in 480 BC. The enumeration of his troops took place at Dorisars, in Thrace, in that year.